Praise
Name, Claim & Reframe

"Andrea shows us that there is enormous value in facing the triggers that keep us from becoming our best selves. With wit and eloquence, she gently nudges us forward, illuminating new perspectives that give us a pathway to our truest power and greatest potential."

> —MACALL GORDON, MA, sleep expert
> and author of *Little Livewires*

"I devoured this book. Andrea's message of self-sovereignty and her manual to bring us back to our truest essence is exactly the message the world needs right now. Filled with specific examples of transformation and change, Andrea helps us return to our truest, most potent power."

> —TRICIA BOLENDER, MBA, CPCC, Executive Coach
> and creator of "Sacred Power" programs

"Andrea Mein DeWitt's call to disarm is a golden nugget that will shine brightly and change the way people live their lives. Breathtaking and thought-provoking, it is a brilliant reminder that it is only when we name our truth that we find the courage to claim ourselves, reframing the way we navigate our lives ever after."

> —BETH CHRISTENSEN, LMFT, Psychotherapy and
> Counseling, Dialectical Behavior Therapy practitioner

"Funny, relatable, insightful, and inspiring. By letting us see her authentic self, the "ah-ha" moments that got her there, and how she's guided her clients to look at things through a different lens, Andrea Mein DeWitt helps us visualize new possibilities and gives us a valuable toolbox for creating our best lives."

> —JULIA HOLIAN, CPC, career strategist and interview coach

"Andrea Mein DeWitt's supportive nature, eloquence and guidance make this book un-put-down-able. The stories sprinkled throughout—both those of clients and her personal ones—not only serve to illustrate how effective the Name, Claim & Reframe concept is, but also drew me in immediately. Every woman deserves to become a gentle warrior and this book is the toolbox she needs to make that happen."

—MELANIE HERSCHORN, MA, coach and business strategist, host of *AUTHORity Marketing LIVE*

"A perfect balance of personal story and coachable elements, DeWitt's energy infuses the reader with the confidence that they can create the world in which they choose to live. DeWitt speaks with authority on the fragility of the mindset of emerging adults and their turbulent life choices, helping them pave the way to less confusion older generations have had to slog through."

—KIM O'HARA, author of *No Longer Denying Sexual Abuse*

"This wonderful, witty, and insightful book presents a tangible formula that will help us address the emotional triggers that hold us back from our most authentic self. Timely, practical, and liberating, *Name, Claim & Reframe* is a welcome roadmap to expand our self-awareness, intention, and mindset strategy from the inside out!"

—MARGARET M. BLANC, MA, LMFT, Psychotherapy and Counseling, holistic health educator, integrative yoga therapist

---

"Andrea offers us a clear, defined masculine structure to live a softer, heart-centered feminine approach to life and has packaged it through her own unique lens and voice. Offering personal anecdotes and examples to ground these teachings, this book, and the stories and tools within it, will invite you to show up to life as your best self."

—ABIGAIL MORGAN PROUT, MA, PCC & Sarah Wildeman, PCC, coaches and co-leaders of Spiral Leaderhip

---

Name
Claim &
Reframe

Name
Claim &
Reframe

YOUR PATH TO A
WELL-LIVED LIFE

Andrea Mein DeWitt

Hatherleigh Press is committed to preserving and protecting the natural resources of the earth. Environmentally responsible and sustainable practices are embraced within the company's mission statement.

Visit us at www.hatherleighpress.com and register online for free offers, discounts, special events, and more.

Name, Claim & Reframe

Library of Congress Cataloging-in-Publication Data is available upon request.

ISBN: 978-157826-958-7

Printed in the United States

10 9 8 7 6 5 4 3 2 1

"Not all storms come to disrupt your life,
some come to clear your path."

— ANONYMOUS

Contents

Foreword

BY TANYA GEISLER

HUMANS ARE FUNNY, AREN'T THEY? We can go our whole lives missing the things that are right under our noses.

Like, say, a book's subject line. In all honesty, I'm not sure I've ever noticed one before I was gifted a copy of the book you are holding in your hands:

Name, Claim & Reframe: Your Path to a Well-Lived Life.

It's a bold assertion, isn't it?

My path? Well-lived life?

What does any of that even mean? Especially now, in the days and years following a global pandemic whose ever-unfolding impact continues to reveal the long-existing cracks in the structural foundations that our society can no longer choose to ignore.

And yet, that's precisely and exactly what this book delivers.

An ACTUAL path to an actually well-lived life.

With a strong framework and deliciously told real-life stories, Andrea takes us THERE.

But first I want to talk about two aspects of the writer and the human that Andrea is.

The first is that she is a delightfully real and generous TEACHER.

She has developed the *Name, Claim and Reframe®* framework over years of lived experience, palpably deep curiosity, and keen analysis from whence you can see her lawyerly roots. But it's the way that she is so keenly committed to making sure what she serves up isn't just *inspirtaintment* (if that's not a word, it is now), but rather is useful, helpful, and immediately applicable. Transformation doesn't happen in the pages of a book... it happens when we take the work out into the world.

The second, paradoxically, is that she is a delightfully real and receptive LEARNER. Woven into every page is a generous attribution to the mentors and teachers who have come into her life, for a reason or a season, and she has curated the best of what she has gleaned in her ever-evolving discovery process.

I am one of those mentors. And it's a deep honour to see my work with the Imposter Complex and leadership development reflected back through the lens of Andrea's experience.

I have witnessed firsthand Andrea taking some key piece of insight offered by another's teaching with open heart, even if she's seen it before, and with both humility and curiosity, metaphorically bringing it up to the light, turning it in her hands to catch the prismatic refraction of new insight and then integrating that into her understanding, and then, teaching.

Now, about that framework.

The very best processes are simple. But let there be no doubt, *Name, Claim & Reframe* will ask of you. It is, as the kids say, #simplenoteasy.

What it offers us, the readers, is choice.

The choice to disrupt our own conditioning and narratives of unworthiness and to decide another way, the way of deepening into the knowing of our innate magnificence and capacity. Or not.

As we collectively look to divest from hustle culture, patriarchal structures and systemic obstacles designed to keep so many folks from climbing to the top, as well as attempt to rebuild those aforementioned shaky foundations, Andrea nudges us firmly and mindfully to a way of embracing the ANDness we all hold.

Which is sweet relief given the fact that the self-development industry clocks in at over $40 billion dollars which is a lot of money devoted to making you feel wrong about yourself.

Nope.

Not here.

She will simply not make you feel wrong.

Andrea invites us to get curious about what is actually happening in a moment. To make some real time choices. And then to move in the direction of what we SAY we want.

But—and here's where it gets *real* good—this involves including our WHOLE selves. Not just the shiny bits. Not just the polished and sanitized and socially desirable bits. But the rough bits, the hard bits, the tender bits, the fierce bits. The bits we've been told to shelve because we're too much and exhaustingly, not enough.

She invites all of that to the party that is our existence.

ALL of ALL of us.

Because in these pages, you will be reminded that you are whole as you are. That your ANDness matters. And that your contradictions are magnetic.

So yes.

My path to a well-lived life includes all of me. And it includes choice.

We have work to do, friends. It won't be easy, but if we can rewrite those internal narratives designed to keep us stuck, remember who we really (really) are, and take aligned action from there in service of the greater good? I have deep faith in us.

I'm excited for you to find YOUR path to a well-lived life too.

Tanya Geisler
Certified Leadership Coach *&* TEDxWomen speaker

Introduction

I AM A WARRIOR IN RECOVERY, HAVING MADE THE INTEN-
tional choice to align with a more feminine approach to life. I would
venture to guess that you wear your own suit of metaphorical armor. It
hides your truths, your false identities, and most importantly, the pain
that you have stuffed away and never acknowledged. You have learned
to cope, sometimes reverting to the same old, stale patterns of the past
that leave you feeling empty and unfulfilled. The overarching message
of this book is to illustrate how the suit of armor that we have built over
our essential selves (Alfred Alder, 1927) has in fact inhibited us from our
most potent power and skewed the balance of the divine masculine and
feminine ingenuity that exists within all human beings regardless of
their gender identity. I call forth a more attuned approach to life when
I speak of "living in the way of the Gentle Warrior." As I understood
the process to become a Gentle Warrior, I came upon the call to help
others disarm and Name, Claim and Reframe their lives. What I present
is not a "healer weekend" as a Gentle Warrior, but rather a new life path
and approach to relationships. If you are ready to shift your mindset
and welcome in a more strategic approach to living a happier and more
fulfilled life, then we have some work to do.

I was a valiant warrior who "handled" everything and everyone who
got in the way of my plan. Does that sound familiar to you? This inflexible and ego-driven mindset left me battle bruised, exhausted, and very
unbalanced, yet I trudged on, afraid to admit that my tendency to lean
into more masculine gallantry was not working. Resistant to change and

wary of letting my guard down, I had dug into my fortress, convinced that the strongest survive by white knuckling it and denying any form of uncomfortable emotion. Yet just as we are beginning to think that we have mastered life, an event, an illness, or an uncomfortable truth knocks us to our knees. It's like being hit by a rogue wave and thrown, ass over teakettle onto a hard sandy beach with sand in your bikini bottoms. We find ourselves disoriented and gasping for breath. Other surges follow and push us into the realization that if we are to survive the impact, we must shift the frequency of who we are and how we approach our life going forward. Our priorities are called to shift, causing false identities and past wounds to rise to the surface. We are rattled and forced to evolve or stay stuck in the limbo that is unfolding. We need a way not to just cope, but to shift our perspective and our mindset. If you have been shaken or dropped into the call for real change, we can make it sustainable and impactful so that you do not have to force yourself or situations in your life ever again. You will wield a new sword, responding to life instead of reacting to it.

Great change is always preceded by chaos and confusion, and our darkest moments have great purpose. If life is bringing you the circumstances you need to emerge into a more authentic version of yourself, then it's time to take hold of a new way of being and transform yourself so you can start embracing adverse experiences instead of resisting them.

To transform to a higher frequency in your life you will have to disarm and step out of your armor so you can meet the Gentle Warrior that exists within you. Man or woman, that warrior is there. It is only when we dare to look inside ourselves that we find the truth to light our way forward. Read on and prepare to be enchanted by your own inner magnificence.

CHAPTER ONE

A Call to Disarm

W E ALL KNOW THAT WOMAN. SHE DOESN'T LEAD WITH an axe or come in with all guns a-blazing to get life done. She elegantly draws upon her own inner resources to guide, counsel, and direct her actions. She stands resolutely in her truths and is one with the most authentic and essential parts of herself.

My encounter with such a woman, Linda, shook the very foundation of my core beliefs, causing me to re-think how I lead in all areas of my life. She was my mentor and through this experience, I started the journey towards building the framework for living life like a Gentle Warrior. I too wanted to walk through decisions in a beautifully feminine, articulate, and witty way, to check my ego at the door and generously strategize so I could lead with an impactful and altruistic vision. Like Linda, I was a straight shooter, however, I was fueled by a lot of triggers, core wounds, and deep seeded insecurities. Many women are.

Building the framework of a Gentle Warrior did not come over night. I had to take a purview of life's ups and downs, from childhood to present, to *Name* how I got here and *Claim* what I wanted. The *Reframe* was a realignment of perspective that provided the vision for me to strategically take my power back. As modern women, we have armored

1

up to protect our soft centers. Most women have not had time to learn or be open to guidance for stopping our fight responses and shedding our armor. To find this champion within yourself, your Gentle Warrior, you must look to the leaders who have boldly embraced a more feminine approach to their lives. It was in the Reframe phase that I found a more intuitive mindset that created more ease and flow in my life. You too have this softer more emotionally attuned side and it holds the secret ingredients to your most potent power, your divine feminine ingenuity. I used to believe that being a confident woman meant that I showed up a bit bitchy, forcing my opinion, and "not taking crap from anyone." Kind of like being a man in a woman's body. But feminine power is so much more interesting, intricate, and intelligent.

Initially in my process, I grew precociously eager, leaping into personal and professional development with grandiose curiosity. I observed colleagues, mentors and thought leaders with awe, wondering what would happen if women as a collective became more comfortable leading with our divine feminine gifts. Working beside and reading the work of many of the ingenious leaders you will encounter in this book, called me forth to investigate the specific qualities that embody strong, thoughtful leadership. Enchanted and excited about what I was learning, I began the practice of disarming from my more masculine driven tendencies and permitting myself to embrace the lady that lives under my warrior. Instead of forcing her power externally, she uses an innate feminine attunement to access her internal power which yields a grace and wisdom built on intuition, connection, and humility. With more awareness around the opportunities we have as women, to support each other and have a deeper understanding of how our emotional triggers often block our ability to stand in our power, I believe that we are at a crucial turning point if we are to break new ground as a united feminine coalition.

Linda, who was fifteen years my senior, had most likely not gotten to where she was without surviving a few storms of her own. Women just like her have put on a brave face to suppress the pain caused by childhood abuse, inequality in the workplace, discrimination, infidelity, illness, and maligned family history, to name a few. Yet despite the challenges in her past, this woman stands comfortably in her own skin and holds her ground with a steady graciousness that hints she could be skilled with sword and shield, but only as a last resort. While I am not saying that we can be conflict-free, detaching from our emotional triggers and defense mechanisms allows us to use emotional expression and communication to raise and diffuse challenging situations. The vulnerability of consciously expressing feelings at work, on a conference call or in the board room is not a weakness, it is a sign of integrity and a strategy that can disarm the arrogant and inspire the reluctant. It is through this earnest connection to our most innate feminine gifts and talents that we gain access to the radiant brilliance that exists within all of us.

The process of becoming a Gentle Warrior is not sudden or easy, but it is well worth your while to learn. Why are we all not looking to access this wise leader within ourselves? We are wearing the wrong armor, donned by generations of women before us who did not understand all the nuances of their own divine feminine gifts. If you would like to use your intuitive hunches to lead and support others with poise and insight, then it is time for a change. If you would like to lean into your emotional intelligence, show up in the world with integrity, creativity, and a willingness to collaborate and communicate with honest sincerity, I have a path through Name, Claim and Reframe.

What are the key traits of a woman who has put down her metaphorical cloak of armor to walk the Gentle Warrior way?

She has an acute awareness around the stability of both her feminine and masculine gifts and understands how to notice and then recalibrate when she is triggered into reacting instead of responding to adverse situations. She is an effective negotiator because she is a good listener, and her empathic abilities help her stay connected to others' needs and concerns. Most importantly, she knows that the best decisions are made with a calm and centered mind, and she is skilled at avoiding that "out of control" feeling that comes when we are energy depleted having pushed past the limits of our sanity.

If all those qualities stir your heart, but you also feel far from stepping into those shoes, then we have some work to do. We all have the capacity to embody our true feminine nature, but have learned over time to deny it because we think that to compete more effectively in a masculine dominated world, we must show up as hardened and armed warriors. We become rigid and inflexible, forcing our hand in an effort to prove we are able, tough-minded, and skilled in the art of male patriarchal warfare. Out of touch with our innate gifts for nurturing others, cultivating connection and resourceful resilience we lose our sense of community. Instead of asking for help, we become territorial, and begin to perceive other women as threatening. We feel isolated, unbalanced, and disheartened, forgetting that our impact yields the most power when we get curious about why we feel disconnected from ourselves. Our answers lie within the emotional triggers and limiting beliefs that keep us chained to unhealthy patterns of behavior.

How did we get here and how can we get back? What would happen if we became more comfortable leading with our divine feminine proficiencies? With more awareness around the opportunities that we have as women to support each other, we are at a crucial turning point if we are to break new ground as a united feminine force. The women who enter my coaching practice often speak of an ache or tug at their heart that suddenly forces them to choose between their truth and life's status quo. They have spent so much time pleasing and supporting others, that they have lost themselves. While they may have clarity on what they do NOT want, they are not sure how to access what they do want.

Although most women who are pulled in a thousand different directions can default to a more masculine sword and shield, a Gentle Warrior has the tools to Reframe her combative approach to life and has adopted a more nuanced integration of herself that showcases her masculine proactiveness with her feminine ingenuity. If you are nodding your head, your armor most certainly bears the dings of life. By bravely disarming, you can transform into an attuned and more powerful revision of yourself. When we choose to stand in the truth of who we are at our core, we open our hearts, becoming more intentional in our actions by creating a community that will support the vision we have for ourselves and the greater good we hope to achieve in the world. I am acutely aware that retaining your strength while opening your heart is easier said than done, yet I have learned that there is an elegant strength that comes from achieving this softer way through life's challenges.

For me and so many other women, the concept of self-sovereignty gives rise to the impulse to boldly take our power back. Whether it is a desire to claim something new for yourself or a life transition that forces you to take action, at any age a woman can "give themselves permission" to start a business, begin a big project, earn that degree, leave a marriage, or even to fall in love all over again. Like a personal check-in, this is the point when women realize that it is time to take up more space and build energetic boundaries that will fill them instead of depleting them. They have a deep yearning to claim something of their very own. While for some, this transition happens slowly over time, like an ache or a longing, for others it feels more like a collision that clears the way for a new beginning that they never saw coming. Whatever your situation, I am here to tell you that learning the way of the Gentle Warrior can only be achieved by opening your heart and intentionally embracing the storm.

Although one traumatic incident is often the passageway to enlightenment, we may be afraid to admit to our stories and the pain we endured because of them. Yet struggle is often the portal to a vast reservoir of inner resourcefulness. Not only are we gifted great wisdom, but we learn of the internal strength that we possess, enabling us to boldly rise again. Life's bruising is inevitable, but enlightenment from the bruising is optional. If we allow ourselves to dig into the truth behind our darkest moments, we will find that we are closer to the spirit of a Gentle Warrior than we might think.

A Wave of Truth

My passage to a higher frequency of self was a sudden and dramatic loss of the feeling of financial stability. I can honestly tell you that I never predicted that a financial crisis would be the incident that would set me free from a life off course, but it was my portal out of the stagnancy of a life that was no longer working. When we are lost, off course and not aligned with our truth, the universe has a way of getting our attention. Maybe the event was sent to help you get out of your own way. Even when we play by the rules, an unexpected wave can destroy our navigation plan, or rather, what we thought it was. Will you be a proactive adventurer, opening your heart to what might be possible? Or will you react by playing the victim and allowing the event to define you?

One spring afternoon, my husband and I discovered that an investment that we believed was "safe" was instead tanking and we needed to pour in more funds than we had readily available to preserve the investment. Growing up, my parents did not teach me very much about money management. What we needed was paid for, and there was rarely financial panic. Going into our marriage, my husband and I both had our own income and had been prudent investors, but I see now in hindsight that I had checked out of the financial conversation, choosing by abstention to ignore the details and leave my husband to do all the worrying and problem solving. Now in a more tenuous place, I needed to look at the cold hard truth of what we were facing. My husband was building a consulting practice after leaving a corporate career and we were very simply spending more than we were making.

We had a fairly high cost of living that included a vacation home and it felt like we were in danger of losing it all. I was angry and afraid. It felt incredibly messy, and I wanted to point fingers, but truthfully, I was at fault too. Because I had been in denial, and not in the conversation with my partner about our financial status, I had willingly surrendered my power. This is a common mistake that many women make, turning the finances over to their spouse without question, despite contributing to the annual income. To face this situation, I had to look at what frightened me most, talking about where we were in the red and taking ownership of my part in my family's financial state of affairs. A Gentle Warrior asks hard questions, shares difficult truths, and is never afraid to reveal her deepest fears.

For the first time in my life, I had to rethink my whole financial value system and the way that I had always responded to money. Due to my comfortable financial upbringing, I had never really had to budget, let alone check for the lowest priced items at the grocery store. I wasn't frivolous, just detached from the bottom line. As my husband explained the whole scope of our financial situation, we considered our options. We could take on more debt to keep our beloved vacation home, but the newly awoken warrior within me screamed a resounding, *"HELL NO!"* As a mortgage banker's daughter, I knew that the only winners in borrowing deals were the lenders. The Universe was giving us another chance and we had it in our vacation home, an asset that could save us. It was a wakeup call that the party was over.

It was like a bad dream, so I dug into my own inner resources and came up with a plan. The sale of our second home would take time, longer than we felt we had to raise the cash we needed. Without telling my husband, I drove over to my parents' home and arranged a bridge loan with the one loan shark that I trusted, my father. It was one of the most courageous, yet strangely, vulnerable things I have ever done. By choosing to become an adventurer, I had taken the helm of our sinking ship. I cannot begin to find the words to express the emotion conjured by this financial challenge - humility, shame, and regret only scratch the surface, but I knew that this storm had come to save us from ourselves. Our financial shock, as scary as it seemed, was not life threatening. It was instead the jolt of reality that would set us free so we could chart a new and more visionary course for the future. I Named the terror of us losing what we had worked so hard to build then I got onto the other side of it so, together we could Claim a solution and begin to navigate our next steps. My husband felt that I had betrayed him when I shared what I had done behind his back, but as we discussed the pros and cons of my parent's help vs. the other options, we eventually agreed it was the most prudent course of action.

Selling our vacation home so suddenly felt like a fire sale and people reacted in strange ways when we told them. As the shame of their bewildered and patronizing glances washed over me, I dug into the reality of the situation: we were lucky to have a second home to sell and it was time to change course and swim to safety. In changing my perspective, I Reframed my thinking. It was time for us to write a new story and leave the life we had been living behind. When you intentionally wake up, serendipity reigns and circumstances fall into place. Our property sold for more than we expected, and we were able to quickly repay my parents and straighten out our finances. Instead of anger at my situation, I Reframed my mindset and chose to feel compassion for my husband who had been navigating this situation alone and for myself for hiding from it. This experience brought us back together as equal partners, restoring trust within our marriage. If we could get through this conflict, we could get through anything.

As corny as it may sound to you, this is when the Gentle Warrior inside me stepped forward. Instead of fighting her way through her problems with sword and shield like I had all my adult life, she chose to lead with love, collaboration, and ingenuity. Part of rebuilding our life again was believing that it was possible to do so. However disgraceful I felt our situation was, I had hope, and trusted that we would rise again. My courage would be the beacon that would light our way through and out of the storm. The key ingredient of partnership is to stand together to see a way forward. I saw our situation not so much as a crisis, but rather an opportunity to get creative and scrappy. By accepting the mess, we were in as a blessed portal to salvation, we had taken control of our lives, Claiming the autonomy that was essential to break new ground and forge a future of our choosing.

Humility has a way of birthing grace, and gratitude flooded our conscientiousness: our love for each other, our health, our children, the home we were able to sell, and my parents who bridged us a loan. Having experienced a financial intrusion called forth a fortitude within me that I had forgotten existed. As I began to accept the situation that we found ourselves in, I mentally Reframed it for what it was, merely a hiccup in my life story. When we stop running from our truths, we can begin to instead look for and Claim the hidden treasure within them. I had the power to shed the shame of my story and use it as an opportunity to reinvent myself, Reframe my identity. I no longer wanted to hide from the things in my life that I felt like I wasn't capable of handling. I wanted to face it all, but without the dread and sheer panic I had experienced through our days in the financial mire. I felt a strong pull from within to rise, stronger and more enlightened with a clearer vision and sense of purpose. The experience of being lost myself felt like a redemption story that I could pay forward. It was also my golden opportunity to create some sovereignty and take my power back, so I made the bold decision to leap, pivoting from an over thirty-year career in education to become what had been calling all along, a certified Life and Leadership Coach. Using my past pain to model, teach and guide, I yearned to be a beacon of hope for others who had lost their way.

In all chaos, there is a secret order that breeds curiosity, versatility, and resourcefulness. Introduce a little anarchy and our brains will find a structure to reorder the chaos. I had found the structure that led me to navigate myself back towards a well lived life: Name, Claim and Reframe.

Once we see our truth, we cannot unsee it. When I finally acknowledged the hardened warrior parts of myself that had dominated my tendencies to react aggressively to adversity instead of responding to it strategically, I emerged more attuned to my core beliefs and met a woman I quite liked. She was comfortable in her skin and didn't need to prove anything to anyone but herself. And the best part, because I got closer to the most authentic and essential parts of myself, my marriage grew stronger. Truth had a way of grounding our relationship in love, honesty, and deep respect for one another. I was falling in love again, not only with my husband, but more importantly, with myself.

The best guides have traveled the path, understand the obstacles, and share humbly from their scars of enlightenment. The experience of being lost myself offered me the road map to develop Name, Claim and

Reframe, or the way of the Gentle Warrior. I understood that anyone could use these three steps at any point in their life, big crises like mine, or everyday micro messes. Anyone who has been knocked to their knees needs to believe that they have the power to rise again and the framework to do so. Whatever disrupts "the who" you thought you were and "the what" you thought was sacred (marriage, health, financial stability), the power to recover lies within you. Maybe your disaster is calling you to become something better than you were before.

Panache Desai wrote: "Often the precursor to spiritual awakening is some crisis, something that cuts through the thick layers of illusion of the ego. (The event) awakens to facilitate the emergence of the transcendent beauty and joy that you could not see in the chaos and perceived limitation . . . You begin to see life with new eyes and an open heart."*

Desai reminds us that the storm has come to wash us clean and that there are valuable lessons in everything, especially the hard things. Wholeness comes not from dancing in sunshine and rainbows, it comes from weathering life's worst storms. How we conduct ourselves through the humility and the vulnerability of adverse situations is in fact what creates Gentle Warriors.

Although it took me a long time to share my embarrassing story publicly, each time I boldly shared my truth, the shame and regret loosened their grip and I saw again that I had found the portal to my own salvation. Now it's your turn. What have you weathered that you feel horrified sharing? This story may in fact be the way through to a new life path. I encourage you to take the first steps in acknowledging

---

* Panache Desai, *You Are Enough: Revealing the Soul to Discover your Power, Potential and Possibility* (2020)

the challenges that you have weathered in life and reflect on why you struggle to share your pain with others.

- How have these challenges impacted your abilities to stand in your power?
- What are the limiting beliefs around this struggle and what mindset shifts might you need to Reframe going forward?
- How might sharing your experience lighten the burden and help forge a path closer to the truth of who you are?

Choosing to share challenges openly, to heal, and to also make a connection with others is the most courageous choice that we can make from a divine feminine perspective. When we disarm and boldly acknowledge our darkness, we begin the process of finding our way through it. Allowing yourself to be received in a safe space of trust is beautifully feminine and the first essential step in becoming a Gentle Warrior.

While you must read on to learn of the healing power of seeing and acknowledging the pain you have concealed under your armor, my hope is that you and other women will be both inspired and encouraged to Name, Claim and Reframe your core limiting stories so that you too can live happier, more fulfilled lives. Then each time you encounter a set-back or disappointment in life, you can have the opportunity to Name, Claim and Reframe the situation. It is through the vulnerability of seeing and feeling our pain, fears, and regrets that we emerge with the ability to Reframe them so we can choose to rise again, a magnificent revision that is closer to the truth within ourselves.

When we take time to respond in a way that reflects our authenticity, we take our power back and become more aligned with the gentle and knowing leader that lives inside of us. It may not always be perfect but knowing that you have choices during difficult times allows you to listen to your heart and live more authentically in your integrity. I see my storm as the blessed incident that provided me the opportunity to choose again. My story is proof that if you are going in the wrong direction, the universe will send a rogue wave to set you back on course.

If we are to pursue a well lived life, the universe will most certainly conspire to assist our evolution to a higher frequency of self. While infidelity, chronic illness, or the sudden death of a loved one doesn't seem to be a blessing, how we choose to weather a setback may in fact be the inciting incident that knocks us back onto our destined course. As you boldly Name the mess you find yourself in, you have two choices: grab the helm and become an adventurer in your own life or sit in the victim's chair and allow the ship to take you down.

CHAPTER TWO

Balancing Your Response

W E BEGIN THE PROCESS OF NAME, CLAIM AND REFRAME by understanding that, as human beings, regardless of our gender identification, we possess and draw upon both masculine and feminine energies. "Energy" can be qualified as the specific character traits that each of us possess and bring to any given situation. Although the polarities of our male and female traits both attract and complement each other, we must learn to decipher their differences, as either energy, when taken to extremes, can transform into poison. Someone leaning too much into one will naturally bring a corresponding decrease in the other and it is this lopsidedness that can undermine even our best intentions. Feminine energy can be described as receptive, gentle, intuitive, and nurturing. Masculine energy is associated with being action-oriented, courageous, forthright, and focused. If we are to achieve the harmony of a well lived life, we must gain awareness of how to balance the best parts of each half of our wholeness. It is a misconception that men "should" present themselves with more masculine traits, while women are expected to present more feminine ones. The truth is that we all embody both masculine and feminine energies and when you begin to notice the interplay of these characteristics in yourself, it will influence not only your mindset but the way you choose to respond to adversity.

Many ambitious women believe that they have no choice but to lean into their masculine characteristics to showcase their power and strength, yet we need to draw from both sides as there are intricacies in our femininity that when applied with grace, wisdom, and resourcefulness yield much more impact and influence. The age-old warring warrior myth that to conquer means to force, kill, or overpower others is yesterday's news. Let me first provide you with some context of the danger of lopsidedness as together we get curious about the gentle, wise, and versatile essence that lives under your protective armor.

A Warrior in Recovery

My childhood home was infused with masculine energy, and at an early age, I learned to armor up, carry my weight, and stuff my emotions. Although my mother made great efforts as a homemaker, I was clearly under the impression that masculine traits were more valuable than feminine ones. My father valued courage, athleticism, and steel equipment. *"You got to be tougher, Annie!"* He would remind me when I teared up after a scrimmage with one of my brothers. Tom Hanks' line in the 1992 film, *A League of Their Own* sums up the energy of my childhood home beautifully: *"Are you crying? There's no crying in baseball!"*

Our father taught us to shoot guns, drive 4x4 vehicles backwards, and ski like Olympic hopefuls. Bruising was expected, and failure was not an option. Not surprisingly, my only choice was to carry a sword and compete with my two younger brothers like a resigned soldier. Adherence to the code of masculinity helped me to acclimate to my childhood home, but as I reached adulthood, my tendency to default to more masculine traits created unnecessary conflict and angst throughout my life. This take no prisoners approach did not serve or showcase the best parts of me, and as I marched on through life with determined focus, I may have even unknowingly intimidated and alienated those I hoped to befriend. Although I was independent, responsible, and proactive, some people just didn't like me, and I couldn't understand why. Trying to please those who clearly are not part of your cheering section leads to self-doubt, victimhood, and passive aggressive behavior. I often felt unbalanced as the courageous and driven parts of me bullied and chastised my feminine side, causing me to be self-deprecating, apologetic, and insecure. You don't need external adversaries to weaken your feminine essence when you have a warrior inside that takes her down at every turn.

The idea of using femininity to navigate life has always been an enigma to me because I got such mixed messages about the power of feminine energy from my mother, Rosemary, who prided herself for being a tomboy. My mother boasted of studying Physical Education in college and teaching high school girls P.E. before I was born. Although she taught just five years, her whole identity was wrapped up in competitive sports like golf and tennis. My mother was flat chested, dressed in 1960s style Laura Petrie capri pants, and bopped around town in a little red Volkswagen Bug. Don't get me wrong, my mother was an attractive woman, but in a sporty, "Twiggy" (the 1960s English style icon) kind of way. She had little time for fussiness in her morning beauty routine, and her cosmetics consisted of sunscreen and her signature red lipstick. The short pixie hair cut she wears today is the same sensible cut she wore in the 1950s when she was in college. My mother's wash and wear hair was a novelty as most other mothers were sleeping in curlers. It suited my mother because she was always running off to "do" something. *I have no time for hairdos,"* she would laugh as she jumped out of the shower and towel dried her hair.

When we were young, our mother used her Irish skin and the need to avoid the sun as an excuse to curate a smart collection of "Great Gatsby" style caps in every color of the rainbow. She looked like Peter Pan with three children in tow, each cap matching one of her sporty, Twiggy, "running out the door" outfits. She had a trim figure and I loved when she dressed up and wore make up, but she was most comfortable dressed in either her tennis skirt or penny loafers and a red cardigan sweater. If you met my mother today, you would behold an impish, sassy, and spunky lady, but not an overly feminine one. I sense that my mother struggled with her own feminine essence because she was raised by only her father. Although she describes her childhood home as a "girl's house," her mother's absence meant that feminine energy was in short supply.

How do you balance your masculine and feminine energies?

Think about your own childhood:

- Who in your life has influenced your masculine traits, either positively or negatively?

- Who in your life has influenced your feminine traits, either positively or negatively?

- What masculine characteristics do you value in yourself?

- What feminine characteristics do you value in yourself?

- What traits, either masculine or feminine, inhibit your ability to stand in your power?

Given my childhood experiences, you won't be surprised that my masculine traits were *assertive, ambitious, driven, direct, confident, independent, analytical, strong, courageous, competitive, protective,* and *disciplined.* Yet my more unsavory masculine traits, *aggressive, dominant, insensitive, territorial, stubborn, rigid,* and *controlling,* came out more frequently at times in my life when I felt threatened or fearful and allowed my masculine warrior to lead.

When I did witness the feminine parts of my mother, they presented themselves in a more negative light: *insecurity, seeking validation, and reactive tears of frustration.* Still, my mother gave us her all, approaching motherhood with fierce loyalty by modeling for herself what "a good mother" does. She cooked balanced meals, encouraged us to participate in activities and then drove us there. She volunteered in our classrooms, advocated for us when we needed support and made each Christmas magical. I instinctively knew that her faithful attentiveness masked great pain because it often bubbled to the surface in strange ways. When she became overwhelmed, she'd tearfully reminded us, *"I didn't have a mother. You have no idea how lucky you are."* If one of us misbehaved, she'd comment, *"I am such a good mother, why are you acting like this?"* When contrasting my father's strong masculinity with my mother's more spartan feminine traits, I deduced that the masculine side of myself might serve me better in life.

As I grew to adulthood, raising children and working full time, I tried to emulate my mother's devotion and pushed myself until I was running on fumes. I wanted to do it all: to be a leader in my profession, volunteer in my children's classrooms, and create the kind of home seen in Martha Stewart magazines. I used grit and all the masculine energy I had witnessed in my childhood to power through those years. I was efficient, direct, and concise, but I lacked the most essential parts of my true essence, my divine feminine soft side. I did not acknowledge my feelings, especially emotional pain, choosing instead to stuff it deep down. This strategy of continuing to march on to avoid grief, hurt, and anger was not effective. I did not gracefully defend my boundaries.

Instead, I allowed offhand comments to trigger my rage, pushing ever harder to prove that I was enough.

I was stubborn and stoic, never asking for help when I needed it. I recall driving to work many mornings shedding silent tears, like I was hanging by a thread and might snap at any moment. I didn't want to ask for help because I believed that doing so would make me appear vulnerable, or worse, I might be rejected and accused of being grossly inadequate. So instead, I just got resentful, more driven, and pricklier, especially to those I loved the most. I may have successfully checked off all the boxes on my daily agenda (believe me, the warrior within me got every task completed!), but I was not always the patient and nurturing leader, mother, or partner that I wanted to be. When I started working part-time, my 8-year-old daughter observed kindly, "*You're much nicer now, Mommy.*" Her comment alarmed me because I knew that she spoke the truth. I had been showing up more as a stressed-out hag, than the nurturing mother that I so wanted to be.

A Deeper Dive into the Polarities of Masculine and Feminine

I see the dualities of masculine and feminine energies as non-binary entities that all humans hold, regardless of their gender identities. Just like the non-binaries that exist in nature (sun and moon, hot and cold, carbon dioxide and oxygen), they serve as the essential and natural equilibrium within our psyches that create stability, symmetry, and harmony. If we are to present as balanced and strategic, we must gain awareness of our "over-the-top" masculine default tendencies and learn to call up our feminine energy to help us counterbalance, so we have the vision to lead from the inside out.

When a person is primarily using masculine energy, some of their behavior might be *assertive, decisive, logical, protective, competitive, determined, structured,* and *target focused.* While these are all incredible traits for survival and to achieve goals in leadership and in parenting, they are masculine traits. They are warrior-like and keep us and those we hope to serve, safe and on target. And, as I illustrated in the story above, too much masculine energy can present as confrontational, inflexible, and intimidating. When we do not enhance these more forceful traits with our softer feminine ingenuity, we are driving a one wheeled chariot, wobbly and underpowered. When a person is primarily using feminine energy, their characteristics might include being *intuitive, cooperative, receptive, empathetic, collaborative, patient,* and *versatile.* While these are traits that offer compassion, altruism, and inclusivity, with too much feminine, we can present as *clingy, defensive, gossipy, or vindictive.* We need masculine energy to push us forward so that we don't get caught playing small and being the victim.

An Inspired Awakening

Discovering a new truth based on someone else's brilliant thinking allows us to expand our horizons and illuminate new applications. My awareness and desire to enhance my perspectives around more strategic feminine leadership was inspired by my work within the Spiral Leadership community and their Spirit's Compass, a tool developed to help women embody more conscious leadership.

The Spirit's Compass has two intersecting lines: a horizontal line that distinguishes between "above the line" and "below the line" behavior* and a vertical line that categorizes these behaviors as either a masculine or a feminine trait:

> "Conscious leaders know where they are at all times in relation to this line. Above the Line can be described as conscious, open, generative, life-affirming, and curious. Below the Line can be described as closed, defensive, degenerative, life-snuffing, and committed to being right. Based on a millennia of survival instinct, we tend to go below the line when we feel threatened, either physically or emotionally, even if the threat isn't real."
>
> —ABIGAIL MORGAN PROUT,
> FOUNDER OF SPIRAL LEADERSHIP

The Spirit's Compass was alluring to me because while it highlighted both masculine and feminine traits, it invited introspection on how I could gracefully swing between both sides of my wholeness while also providing a structure to gain awareness of situations that triggered my lopsidedness and energy imbalances. The provocative notion that one could consciously Name reactive behavior before it got out of hand and then choose to Claim a response that better matched their truth was revolutionary.

* Adapted from *The 15 Commitments of Conscious Leadership,* Chapman, Dethmer and Klemp (2014)

"'Am I above the line or am I below the line?'" We suggest that the first mark of conscious leaders is self-awareness and the ability to tell themselves the truth. It matters far more that leaders can accurately determine whether they are above or below the line in any moment than where they actually are."

AN EXCERPT FROM *The 15 Commitments of Conscious Leadership*

For a warrior in recovery, there was integrity to these models and an opportunity for me to explore not only the intricacies of how masculine and feminine characteristics impact leadership but also how our actions and reactions trigger us to dip below the line. My curiosity ignited, I set to work using the Spirit's Compass and Chapman, Dethmer and Klemp's brilliant work from "The 15 Commitments of Conscious Leadership," as a foundation of inspiration for Balance Your Response. This tool is the cornerstone of the Name, Claim and Reframe structure: Naming triggers, Claiming resonant actions and Reframing thinking using the horizontal markers of "Above the line" and "Below the line" as the check and balance touchpoint to achieve both balance and wholeness.

Author's Note: The list presented in Balance Your Response is by no means complete or set in stone. Use your own creativity add to, delete, or modify the traits that resonate for you.

BALANCE YOUR RESPONSE

MASCULINE TRAITS

ABOVE THE LINE — NATURAL RESPONSE

Action-Oriented	Influential
Advocate	Integrity
Analytical	Logical
Assertive	Magnetic
Balanced	Mentor
Concise	Objective
Committed	Ownership
Competitive	Physical Strength
Confident	Proactive
Courageous	Problem-Solver
Decisive	Protector
Deliberate	Questioning
Direct	Risk-Taker
Determined	See Possibility
Disciplined	Self-Assurance
Entrepreneurial	Speak-Up
Efficient	Strong
Expansive	Structured
Focused	Responsible
Forthright	Target-Focused
Goal-Oriented	Task-Oriented
Hard-Edge	Thinker
Honorable	Trustworthy
Independent	Visionary
Inner Strength	

FEMININE TRAITS

ABOVE THE LINE — NATURAL RESPONSE

Accountability	Gentle
Adaptable	Generosity
Altruistic	Grace
Attuned	Gratitude
Authentic	Humanity
Beauty	Humble
Celebration	Humor
Cheerleading	Inclusivity
Clarity	Innovator
Collaborative	Inspire
Commitment	Intuitive
Compassion	Loving
Community	Listener
Creative	Motivate
Cultivate	Nurturing
Experience	Open-Minded
Curious	Playful
Delegating	Receptive
Devoted	Resourceful
Ease	Responsive
Emotional	Sensitive
Emotional	Tenderness
Intelligence	Versatile
Empathic	Vulnerability
Empowering	Wisdom
Flexible	

BELOW THE LINE — WOUNDED RESPONSE (Masculine)

Abuse of Power	Inconsiderate
Aggressive	Inflexible
Anger	Insensitive
Arrogant	Intimidating
Assigning Blame	Need-to-be-Right
Autocratic	Negative
Avoidance	Non-Collaborative
Blame/Shame	Overpowering
Boastful	Patronizing
Callous	Pressuring
Close-Minded	Prideful
Confrontational	Rebellious
Controlling	Rigid
Criticism	Silencing Others
Defensive	Stubborn
Destructive	Territorial
Dominating	Undermining
Disconnected	Unstable
Ego-Driven	Unsupportive
Evasive	Verbally Abusive
Grab and Take	Violent

BELOW THE LINE — WOUNDED RESPONSE (Feminine)

Avoidance	Judgmental
Bitchy	Manipulative
Burned-Out	Nervous
Catty	Negative Self-Talk
Clingy	Over-Explaining
Clique/Exclusive	Over-Sensitive
Co-Dependence	Overwhelmed
Compare-Despair	Paralyzed
Compartmen-	Passive
talization	Passive-Aggressive
Complaining	People Pleasing
Cowardly/Fearful	Perfectionist
Dependent	Reactive
Frivolous	Risk-Averse
Fussy	Seeking Validation
Gossipy	Superficial
Haughty	Timid
Impulsive	Vague
Inconsistent	Victim
Indecisive	Vindictive
Insecure	Whiny
Irrational	Withholding
Jealous	

On the upper left side, I have listed what I consider to be natural masculine responses, while on the upper right side, I have noted traits I consider to be naturally feminine. Natural masculine and feminine traits are "above the line" responses because they are positive and promote harmony. As I alluded to earlier in this chapter, leaning too much into one side or the other can convert to a poisonous or wounded response. If you look at the descriptions in the "below the line" quadrants, you find that they are more negative or reactive in nature.

Let's dive into the chart as there is great insight in exploring both the light and dark sides of your wholeness.

Get out a piece of paper and draw four quadrants with a line separating the top from the bottom. Use the top two squares to write your personal above the line masculine and feminine traits. Use two lower squares to list any below the line or wounded responses you have been known to exhibit on either side of your masculine and feminine.

Now take a look at the upper right side (your above the line feminine characteristics), what traits do you see in yourself?

In a perfect world, we would all choose to default to our above the line feminine qualities, but life will most surely cause us to dip below the line from time to time. When you push on to investigate your subterranean, below the line, characteristics, you may find that in the past, you have self-sabotaged yourself with reactive behaviors like being *irrational, passive-aggressive, insecure, over-sensitive, fearful, jealous,* or *haughty.* These self-doubting, mean-girl qualities are all energy depleting and do not showcase the best sides of me, or you, for that matter. Over the next week or so, I encourage you to become an observer in your own life using what you have learned from the Balance Your Response model to notice what situations trigger you to react instead of respond.

When you begin to lean into a new mindset around noticing whether you are in masculine or feminine, you may find that your harder edges have concealed and blocked you from the truest parts of your inner resourcefulness. As Joseph Campbell said, "The cave you fear to enter holds the treasure you seek."

Like finding lost treasure, the Balance Your Response Chart will expand your awareness and help you to get comfortable standing in the more vulnerable heart-centered parts of yourself that you may have hidden away for decades. I have made a practice of using this chart as a check-in tool, especially when I am feeling unbalanced and drained of energy. My adult daughter, Kate, and I have even joined forces, laughing, and reminding each other when our actions and/or comments "dip below the line," into the wounded zone.

"Mom, don't you think that snarky remark sounds a bit judgmental?" or *"I'm not sure why her actions are triggering me. I'll need to reflect on it and bring my thinking back above the line."*

This paradigm shift has helped us both to gain awareness of how to access the best of our inner resources, while also reminding us that unsavory, below the red line behaviors, do not showcase our light, our love, or the legacy we hope to emulate out in the world.

Below are some prompts, I invite you to become a curious observer in your own life.

- What kind of masculine and feminine energy do you want to call in?

- What below the line energies do you want to cast off?

While embodying each of our above the line traits can be both positive and productive, there is an interesting contrast between the two sides—masculine energies are primarily about "doing," while feminine energies reflect "being." While we all must "do" to create momentum in our lives, when we have the mindset of "being," we are more expansive and receptive to the world around us. It is about stopping to reflect and then asking yourself what outcome will best serve the future you hope to create:

- Who do I want "be" in this situation
- What are my short-term goals?
- What other options might serve the legacy I want to leave long-term?

Sometimes we might have to lose small scrimmages, like proving that we are "right" or trying control someone else's agenda, to ultimately win the war within ourselves. In other words, when you feel the urge to *dip below the line*, ask yourself if reacting just to "get your way" will serve you in the long run.

Instead of forcing, controlling, and undermining, this is an invitation to reflect on long term outcomes so you can be strategic in choosing your actions (or inactions) more intentionally. It is only when we slow down, step back and look at the bigger picture that we find resourceful and visionary solutions closer to the truth of who we are at the core. I realize that this concept might alarm a more masculine driven woman, because I used to be her. My warring-warrior-self would push the agenda with the short-term goal of getting my way and then feel depleted, even though I had "won" the scrimmage and proved myself right. But I've learned that there is a more intelligent way through life's challenges.

Below are my Gentle Warrior thinking prompts for you:

- What if you didn't have to push and shove to get what you wanted?
- What if stopping to reflect helped to build both connection and community with those you hoped to influence?

- What if this dance between the two halves of your wholeness helps you to create more flow, harmony, and clarity in your life?

All of this is possible, and the process is the greatest lesson for any Gentle Warrior in the making!

Many of my female clients come to coaching with rigid judgments around letting their emotions show, especially at work. As we dive deeper into the attuned insight behind these emotions, we learn that their gifts of compassion, a desire to connect with others, and the ability to be receptive and supportive of another's ideas are, in fact, the qualities that make them good at what they do.

The work we will do with Name, Claim and Reframe will have you wanting to explore your feminine qualities because it will lead to much more ease and flow in your life. When you give yourself permission to let go of past conditioning and allow a more natural feminine response, your confidence soars because you are suddenly able to access the best parts of yourself, especially when it comes to getting closer to the Gentle Warrior within.

A client, Tori, called me one day in tears, after she and her daughter had a heated political argument. Tori was not only angry but hurt because she and her daughter hadn't spoken in weeks, each so stubbornly rooted in her own views that they had lost sight of the bigger picture. Although she had caught herself, Tori admitted that she had dipped below the line in both her masculine (stubbornly trying to control an outcome) and feminine (judging another's opinion) categories.

"What's the most important outcome for you here?" I asked her. "Do you want to be right or do you want to build a bridge?"

"I want to have an honest, loving and open relationship with my daughter," Tori replied.

We talked about how Tori might extend an olive branch by leaning into her feminine side: humbly apologizing for her part of the argument and agreeing to disagree. When Tori decided not to force her own views onto her adult daughter, she laid down her sword, and embraced a plan fueled more by a feminine energy that was both proactive and ultimately healed the impasse and repaired the bridge with her daughter.

Tori received freedom and fulfillment from simply shifting her energies. You can experience the same in life if you dance more in your feminine essence, or what I like to call, your sweet spot. There is a fine line between the right amount of masculine or feminine energy and the triggering event that takes over to the dark side of imbalance.

The beginning of a Gentle Warrior's journey is to practice both awareness and compassion. Sometimes "doing something" means sleeping on it, taking a warm bath, or calling in for reinforcements in the form of a trusted friend or colleague. Begin slowly by creating space for yourself to reflect on what you might be feeling or what about the situation is especially triggering:

- What do you notice about your response to the situation?
- Would you place your emotion above or below the line?
- Was it a masculine or feminine response?

Giving ourselves permission to step back from a challenging situation helps us to sort through what is most important so we can gain clarity and find a more balanced path towards a peaceful solution within ourselves. We cannot hide from our emotions and if we choose to show up in the world authentically, we have to reconcile with both sides of ourselves to step into wholeness. Tori not only mended a bridge, but she also added a new lane where there was space for tolerance, respect, and more expansive thinking.

The journey of synthesizing and integrating the masculine and feminine of your Gentle Warrior is a process that requires patience, curiosity, and self-compassion. It is the erosion of old thinking that gives way to a more heart-felt ingenuity that leads with generosity, intricacy, and intelligence. As women, we cannot Claim the truest parts of our power until we do the deeper work of understanding our relationship with all the components that make us whole, both male and female. It is never too late to begin the process of seeing your own duality. Having awareness around how to balance the opposing forces of both our masculine and feminine characteristics leads to a more strategic and intentional approach to life. It is not about giving up power, but rather acknowledging the conscious act of enhancing it. A Gentle Warrior does not underestimate the impact of her feminine power and its benefits, nor does she deny the steely masculine parts of herself. She sees each side as an essential part of her integrity and has chosen to dance *curiously* between the two. Every woman possess her own special sauce, and we need YOURS if we are to Claim the fierce majesty of our collective divine feminine potency and authority.

As I have gained clarity about myself and who I want to be going forward, I have combined both my father's masculine confidence with my mother's fierce maternal devotion. I love them both with all my heart and understand more fully now that each side was an essential part of solidifying my wholeness, not only as a leader, but as a woman, a mother, a partner, and a friend. Reconciliation with yourself is the first big step in Claiming the way of the Gentle Warrior.

CHAPTER THREE

Name

"The cure for pain is in the pain. Good and bad are mixed.
If you don't have both, you don't belong with us."

—RUMI

THE FIRST STEP INTO BECOMING A GENTLE WARRIOR IS TO
Name our core wounds and the false identities that we wrap
around them. As you learned in the previous chapter, our tendency to
mask our pain, fear and vulnerabilities leads to an imbalance of blocked
masculine and feminine energy that can restrict us from our natural
resources and keep us attached to limiting beliefs about who we are at
the core. The way to that balance is to start Naming the things of our
past that may have kept us from stepping into the person we want to be
or stated another way, our power and potential.

We work so hard to live within the false identities of ourselves that
we fail to acknowledge the perpetuation of our core wounding, further
discounting our suffering and the recurring themes that continue to
build on top of the initial wound. It's like stuffing everything you don't
want anyone to see back into a shadow-version of yourself, which is why
I often refer to these false identities and core wounds as the shadow-version of oneself.

Women wonder why they work harder to do more and be more, yet their success continues to feel incomplete. Naming is the first courageous step in acknowledging that your false identities were created to battle the shame, hurt, or pain of a core wounding. *I need to be fierce and not feel if I am to be powerful.* Women are tired of this model. We want a new way of navigating a fulfilling life.

As children, we may not comprehend why our parents or role models do not approve of some parts of us, nor do we possess the maturity to understand the pieces of ourselves that we discreetly hide to make the grown-ups happy. Here is where false identities are born as the gatekeepers to the parts of us that are not meant to be known or seen. We stuff them ever deeper into dark shadows of ourselves until we keep bumping up against the same problems and patterns in our lives that hold us back from what we really desire.

Once we Name our false identities, we also "Name the core wound," and call it out for what it is: a roadblock that we must bravely look in the eye in order to heal. The longer you fight to ignore uncomfortable feelings, the longer they will haunt you and stand in your way. When we accept our suffering by understanding the why behind it, we illuminate the dark enigma of the shadow-version that we created for ourselves, by welcoming past pain and suffering into the healing space of our heart.

Facing Our False Identities

Coming to terms with a false identity, "I've got two left feet," "I'm socially awkward," "I'm much too loud," is to Name how it impacted the way you showed up in the world. Your behavior is a direct reflection of what you believe about yourself. The good news is that when you Name a false identity that no longer serves you, that very action puts change into motion. Some of the identities that we carry around, either self-imposed or put upon us through external sources, do not enhance our growth and are fundamentally false—they are merely labels or limiting beliefs we have created due to societal norms, culture, our parents, etc. When you identify too closely with something that simply isn't true, you shut yourself off from change, new perspectives, and growth. Below are some examples of false identities that, left unnamed, could prevent someone from stepping into their power.

Do you see yourself in any of these?

"I'm too emotional."

"My ideas don't matter."

"I'm not the intellectual type."

"I'm a follower, not a leader."

"My energy is too much for others."

"I must stay small and not take up space."

"I can't disappoint others."

"I'm responsible for everyone else's feelings and I need to sacrifice my own."

"It is my responsibility to control outcomes and keep things running smoothy."

"I'm not good at _____." (fill in the blank, the possibilities are endless)

None of these false identities enhance who we are, they were simply stories or limiting beliefs that, over time, we have allowed ourselves to believe. When we begin to Name these identities that we have taken on, we start the process of healing and understanding that they have inhibited our ability to access the truest parts of our power.

> "Your core wounding is separation from self-love, which results in deep feelings of unworthiness. The healing of that wounding is a journey back to your Essential Self."

> —PANACHE DESAI, YOU ARE ENOUGH

When you adopt an identity based on someone else's expectations, or an outdated expectation that no longer fits, you drift farther away from the authentic parts of your essential self, your Gentle Warrior. Naming is the first step in acknowledging that some of the identities, themes, and patterns of the past no longer align with the goals, values, or vision you have for the future you hope to create.

Our false identities have power over us because we believe that we need them to keep us safe from being mentally harmed. While we keep the truth of our essential selves hidden, our ill-fitting identities leave us with a nagging, unexplainable, restless belief that we are somehow not whole. We get comfortable in our false broken-ness and all of its matching wounded behavior traits, and yet we have a feeling that something is wrong. We succumb to the inner voices and critical thinking that are a by-product of the repression of our erroneous identities because we don't know any better. We go so long as our inauthentic selves that the thought of revealing who we truly are brings up fear of being judged or shunned. We have operated within these self-imposed barriers for so long that we have become trapped inside them and even afraid of what we might learn if we dare to look at the truths that they conceal.

Carrie, a CPA with altruistic leadership skills, carried around the core wound that she was a mean person for decades. The identity was bestowed upon her by her father, who called her "mean" when she parented her younger sister.

"I realize now that I may have been a bit bossy to my little sister." she explained, "but my sincere intent was to nurture my sister, not to overpower her."

Carrie didn't really think she was mean, but keeping the false identity fueled the possibility that her father was right. Although Carrie went out into the world with the stigma of mean, she was constantly over-modulating to compensate so she would not "project" the identity of mean. Her reluctance to not appear domineering meant that Carrie did not step into her full essence, which diminished her power and dimmed her leadership impact. In truth, her fear of appearing "mean" clouded her ability to see the light she brought to the world as an altruistic collaborator with a natural ability to guide and inspire others. As Carrie bravely revealed that she worried others saw her style of leadership as "mean," she allowed herself to look at the facts and update an old story with a more current one. Carrie was anything but mean. As we continued to unpack Carrie's false identity, she Named her generous heart that delighted in opportunities to guide and mentor others. As she reflected further, Carrie shared a laundry list of ways that she had subconsciously leaned into nurturing roles in an effort to detach from the identity of "mean." Carrie had been a zoo tour guide in high school, a camp counselor during college, and presently she served as an alumni advisor to active members of her national sorority. Carrie even headed up the onboard training team at her accounting firm. This evidence certainly did not support her father's outdated label of "mean."

"I love working with college women," she mused. "They inspire me to show up as a better version of myself and these younger women offer perspectives about life that I might never have considered."

Through our work, as Carrie began to give herself permission to shed "mean," she embraced her younger self, "Little Carrie," revealing her blocked energy and opening a passageway out of that false identity. Carrie's gut told her that she was very different from the "Little Carrie" tag she had worn for decades, and she longed to shed "mean" so she could update it with a perception of herself that would serve her and the leadership she hoped to project out into the world.

There is a gradual release that begins when we Name our false identities. We unearth a self-limiting belief or fear brought on by a past core wounding. We also allow ourselves to Name an identity that no longer fits who we are, or hope to become. Now that the naming process had occurred for Carrie, we could go back to the masculine and feminine chart and swap out "mean," a below the line masculine trait, for an above the line feminine superpower: *altruistic*. This new perspective also allowed us to dive deeper into areas in Carrie's life where she had been so focused on altruism to service of others that she had unknowingly given too much of herself and drained her internal resources. For Carrie, this simple revision of seeing her energy imbalances unveiled not only a gift that she needed to see in herself, but the wisdom inside her pain to heal a core wound and begin the practice of balancing both sides of her wholeness.

When clients come to me as a coach, I have the honor of witnessing them Name, for the first time, some of the false identities and beliefs that no longer fit who they are. These precious confidences, shared bravely from one to another, are often ill-fitting and sorely outdated. As we pull their false identities out to explore their origin and misconception, clients discover that the labels they have been branded with are often rooted in unsubstantiated facts and memories that are both scant and futile. As we dive deeper, illuminating their sometimes-subconscious attempts to separate themselves through overachievement, avoidance, and self-sabotaging behavior, they find that the path out of their suffering lies within themselves. We never allow ourselves to stand in our own light or to consider how our false identities and core wounds might obscure the gifts we have to offer to the world.

I am not immune to the wearing of false identities, some impacted not only how I saw myself, but also some of my life choices. The first very false identity I held was the secret that I was dumb because I couldn't learn to read. My second-grade teacher, the esteemed Mrs. Hubbard, implanted this thought when she called me out into the hallway, stuck her stern face very close to mine, and said accusingly, "Why do you hate reading?" Her anger shocked me and, as silent tears formed in my eyes, she continued to expand on my crime: "Reading is meant to be loved and YOU aren't trying hard enough to learn."

Her accusations stung because they were untrue. I loved the idea of reading so much that I carried around books that were much too difficult for me to read. The truth was I had a learning disability, a processing disorder that inhibited my ability to hear the individual sounds within words, making it challenging to decode unknown vocabulary. Mrs. Hubbard's accusation wounded me with the false identity that I was not scholarly, that I was dumb, and left a secret sprout of self-doubt that has infested me for decades. I hid my false identity of being dumb by over-compensating; I studied harder than all the other students and became a radical over-achiever. But here's the wisdom or genius (Hendricks, 2018) within this false identity of negative thinking, it became a calling. Because I didn't want other children to feel as I had, I studied elementary education in college, went on to graduate school and became a reading specialist. Whether conscious or unconscious, my career choice, which involved teaching emergent readers, was an attempt to disprove Mrs. Hubbard's accusations, hence soothing the pain of my core wound and the false identity of being dumb. In recent years, I have been able to

Name this false identity, proving that Mrs. Hubbard was quite mistaken. Becoming a teacher who understood how to nurture reluctant readers pointed me towards the why behind my struggle. It also gifted me with a unique insight that fostered an interest in guiding others as a teacher, mentor, and coach. Gay Hendricks, author of *The Joy of Genius* writes that for our genius to emerge we must first free up mind space from the negative thinking of our past: "The biggest barrier blocking our path to genius is fear based negative thinking. Putting an end to the habit is a powerful investment in our genius. Paradoxically, our struggle with negative thinking only ends when we declare we have no control over it."

Where can you give yourself permission to acknowledge the past erroneous false identities you have wrapped around the core wounds of your past due to another's belief about you? Once you Name the source of the belief, you can redirect its impact, choosing to draw out only the wisdom, what Hendrick's calls the genius within the wounding.

Every person has wounds. It's part of the human experience and truthfully, what makes us all unique and interesting. Yet the core wounding that happens in childhood can have potent impact on how we see ourselves. If we can seek it out, there is medicine inside our wound and it is this wisdom (what Hendricks calls, genius) within this shadow-version of self that has the potential to propel us forward to choose certain career paths or to advocate for others that mirror our past suffering. While achieving goals can certainly help to right a wrong or patch up a regret from an earlier life experience, we have to shed light on our false identities, understand our pain and learn "to be with it" (our trauma, resentment, anger, fear, and rejection). Uncovering what the self-sabotaging voice, our inner critic (Kimsey-House, Kimsey-House, Sandahl and Whitworth, 2011) has latched on to, is the only way to repair its damage on our psyches. It is through the arduous process of Naming the wound that has fueled our false identity that causes it to release its grip on our lives. Instead of resisting it, we accept it and offer it love. As hard as it may be to journey into the darkest parts of our shadow selves, there is deep learning and insight inside our wounding, we just need to be brave enough to extract it.

My dear mother, Rosemary's, core wounding was that she was unlovable, brought on by my grandmother, Mary's, absence. Mary, who suffered from severe manic depression, spent most of my mother's childhood in a mental institution. Understandably, Rosemary has guilt about the ambivalence she feels towards her mother, who left when Rosemary was just three years old. Believing that there is shame in mental illness, my mother has never allowed the false identity of "unlovable daughter" to be seen, let alone understood it as abandonment, rejection, unworthiness, and the self-limiting belief that somehow her mother did not love her. The reality was that my grandmother was mentally ill, overwhelmed by depression and unable to function as an adult, let alone a loving parent. My mother's recollections of her childhood are disjointed and vague, sometimes with whole parts missing:

> "I remember, my mother came home for a while right before her youngest sister's wedding, but it didn't last long, she had another breakdown and had to go back to the hospital."
> "You know that's why my father sent us to boarding school in Los Angeles. I was only six and that's when I started to stutter."
> "I remember my father's sisters whispering to each other about my mother, 'What's wrong with her?' We'd hear them say. My sister and I didn't understand any of it and no one explained what was wrong with my mother."

Although these memories are sparse and without much context, when I was growing up, all I could gather was that my grandmother was a tragic figure whose illness prevented her from caring for her children. Core wounds can become generationally layered, and as they are passed quietly down from one generation to the next, we may even find ourselves to be the unknowing hostages of our parent's demons. On the outside, my mom presented the image of a very present and doting mother, choosing to salve her wounds by becoming the overzealous and devoted parent she wished Mary had been. Still, my mother ignored all evidence of her false identity of an unlovable daughter and, to this very day, her ability to reconcile with her core wounding remains a slow and painful process. When she speaks about my grandmother, my mother tears up. There is deep regret and sadness for the loss of this maternal presence, Mary's mysterious absence still an enigma of disgrace. Rosemary knows little about the essence of her mother and Mary's maternal incompetence is what binds the false identities of my mother's core wounds.

Although Carrie and my mother are different ages, they both had been emotionally trapped inside false identities that held them back from the most authentic parts of themselves. Naming our core wounds and false identities helps us to separate from the person we had been told that we are and start living in alignment with the person we are choosing to become. Without this exploration, we are destined to continue to default to the repeated patterns that block our energy and inhibit our ability to heal and see ourselves as whole.

Women often come to my coaching practice because they suddenly notice that the patterns of their past do not fit their hopes for the future. New perspectives about what they want in their lives are beginning to rub up against the traditional beliefs and false identities that have surrounded them for decades. They are attached to certain leadership qualities that they want to emulate, yet they feel stuck and are unsure of how to access them. Over the years they may have adopted the belief that they had to be tough to demonstrate strength and so they are reluctant to show emotion, seeing it as a weakness. As we discussed in Chapter Two, blocked feminine energy leads to even more stuck-ness and below the line wounded responses. In order to create change, we must be willing to lose the outdated parts of ourselves, so we find our divine feminine essence and live closer to our truth. As I have asked myself, many times:

What is it about standing in our feminine power that we fear so much?

Are we worried we will become too powerful and scare those we love with the truth of who we really are?

Author Diane Mariechild's quote makes it pretty clear why God trusted the fairer sex to not only carry the babies, but to birth a new way of being, naturally feminine: "A woman is the full circle. Within her is the power to create, nurture and transform."

A client, Tina, decided she was tired of the identity of "fat lady." In one of our first sessions, she shared the humiliating experience of an angry man in a parking lot yelling, "Hey, fat lady why are you taking up two spots?" The encounter had been so shamefully triggering to her deeper wound of unworthiness that Tina bravely decided that her life needed a bold retrofit: "I am done being defined this one-dimensional identity. It's time for me to take control of my life and how I am living it."

By calling out a disempowering belief that did not serve her, Tina gave herself permission to take her power back and explore the multi-faceted woman that was ready to claim herself again. Together we set to work reshaping Tina's mindset and the areas in her life where she often gave her power away, at work, within her family of origin, and out in the world. Tina set up structures around her energetic boundaries, experimenting with new ways to say a kind but resolute *"no thank you"* or a firm, *"Hell NO!"* She also saw for the first time how the voice of her inner critic often colluded with her feelings of unworthiness and how she might begin to break old patterns of behavior and curate new ways of being and doing. Simultaneously, Tina also enrolled in a physician sponsored weight loss program that offered metabolic counseling, weekly accountability and daily routines that would help her kick start sustainable nutrition habits. She went all in and over the course of a year safely lost over 85 pounds. As she took control and began to curate the way she wanted to live, Tina built new habits, new beliefs and new alliances that conjured both fortitude and confidence. It was a radiant transformation and Tina glowed with the innate radiant beauty that had been obscured by an ill-fitting identity that she had hidden in the secret of emotional eating. Tina started asking herself who she wanted to be now that she was more attuned with her mind, body, and spirit. Her clothes and the activities she chose reflected this change, as she embraced exercise as a new release for managing stress. She joined a hiking group and met like-minded people, shedding old relationships that did not serve who she was becoming. She also rediscovered the sensual part of her femininity and bravely opened her heart to the possibilities of attracting a partner that fit her new beliefs about herself. As her coach, I had the honor of witnessing Tina release what was once stuck energy and transform herself into sassy and sexy woman who stood loud and proud in the true essence that lived at her core.

Naming false identities is about neutralizing negative energy and freeing yourself from the painful emotions that are triggered inside the stale old stories we have unknowingly accepted as true. If we are brave enough, the identity that we created to be the most effective warrior can be a portal to the past that will help us transform the future. Arie de Geus said, "No problem can be solved from the same level of consciousness that created it." It is only by embracing, understanding, and naming our pain that we create the opportunity to dissolve it. Any conflict that is met with compassion, love, and acceptance leads to freedom. Make peace with your hidden parts, as in them lies the roadmap to becoming a Gentle Warrior. It is when we dare to enter the darkness of our shadow-self that we find the radiance to light our way forward.

Core Wounds and Their Triggers

Behind every false identity lies a deeper core wound, formed by an inciting incident—a trauma, a negative experience, or the unsavory label that sprouts a limiting belief. It's all stuck energy that we shamefully conceal within a false sense of self. Over a lifetime, like a dirty wash and rise cycle, the pain of a core wound is triggered over and over again with situations that mirror the emotion conjured by the initial wounding. As counter intuitive as it seems, the antidote to heal the infection of our wound lies in acknowledging its power over us. When we see and sit with what hurt us, we Name the wound and free ourselves and the stuck energy that has kept us from moving forward. Carrie's secret of being "mean" concealed her initial wound of seeing herself as unkind and domineering. My false identification of being dumb, concealed the wound of being seen as inadequate, and my mother's secret of being abandoned by her mother, concealed a wound of being unlovable.

We can't heal what we don't feel. To continue to Name, you must summon the courage to go back to the scene of the crime. What wounded you?

As painful as it may be, half the battle of Naming our core wounds is noticing the feelings that they trigger inside us. We are conditioned to pull away and run from pain, recoiling from the memories that we are mortified to sit with. Whether people want to admit it or not, everyone has something going on that they are not dealing with, and the core of that issue was established from our essential self that felt like we did not belong somewhere in our childhood. While some of us may not remember what happened exactly, there was some sort of emotional disruption that imprinted you with a birthmark of stuck energy.

Author's Note: As a Certified Professional Life Coach (International Coaching Federation and The Co-Active Institute), it is important to state here that Life Coaches are not trained or licensed to diagnose or treat mental health issues. The discussion below of the four categories of core wounding is broad and used only as an overview to create context for "Naming Triggers."

Each one of us has experienced one of these four core wounds at some stage during our childhood:

- **Abandonment.** "There's something wrong with me"; "I'm unlovable"; "I am unimportant"; "I do not feel safe to trust others"
- **Betrayal.** "I am unworthy"; "I am hopeless"; "I am a failure"
- **Physical/sexual/mental/emotional abuse.** "I am ugly"; "I deserve only bad things"; "I'm not in control"; "I am weak"; "I am always unsafe"; "I deserve to be punished"
- **Rejection.** "I am shameful"; "I am a bad person"; "I don't deserve love"; "I have to be perfect"; "I will never belong"

Core wounds originate though our childhood experiences and unfortunately stick with us through adulthood. Also referred to as "emotional triggers," incidents in our adult lives can reopen an old wound even if the incident it is not directly related. Whatever the event, as a young child you did not feel safe, and it imprinted a deep sense of unworthiness that entered you at the core and weighed you down with a heavy dose of shame and guilt. The initial blow was then followed by similar experiences, or what I call "the dirty wash and rise cycle." The experiences began to pile up, solidifying the general feeling that you were not deserving of the virtues that life had to offer. This feeling of unworthiness is called a *core wound* and it impacts you and how you see your life ever after. The good news is that with awareness we can learn to notice and pivot your mindset when they show up in our lives.

The Invisible Girl with the Wayward Hair

The inciting incident that solidified evidence of my inadequacies was my father's dislike of my hair. My long chestnut hair was always in places it didn't belong, in the drain crevasses of my father's sailboat or on the floor mats of his Mercedes. When I was a little girl, I wanted more than ever to have my father to myself, but my thick hair annoyed him. I dealt with this concern by sitting very still and making no noise, praying that my hair would stay on my head and not ignite his anger. This never worked, and on Saturday mornings, when he'd take me to the marina where he tinkered on his sailboat, try as I might, my hair would end up where it didn't belong. I'd cringe, waiting for him to explode, enraged when he discovered one of my rogue locks.

"Damn it, Andrea, your hair is everywhere!" He would bellow.

I would tear up, tuck my pigtails into my jacket, and retreat to a quiet corner of his boat to grow smaller and wait until he found another of my wayward hairs on the dashboard of his beloved German import. At the tender age of eight, I savored any opportunity to spend time alone with my father since he didn't pay much attention to me otherwise. I knew that in order to be in his presence, I had to be invisible and leave no trace of my existence. Being "the invisible girl with the wayward hair" was the false identity fueling my core wound of inadequacy.

Even when we have awareness of how to Name our false identities, the residual effects of our core wounding continue to present themselves as we navigate life and old triggers from our past rear their ugly heads. Naming is the act of catching yourself before you default to the old habit of dipping below the line when a triggering event taps into a core wound. The trigger isn't necessary attached to the event itself, it is instead connected to the emotion you felt way back at the time of your core wounding. It's like an old football injury that never properly healed, it's going to nag you again and again until you take the time to Name the wound and heal it with compassion and grace. I am like a barefoot cobbler, although I am a skilled facilitator of tools and practices to help my clients Name their pain, I still find ways to avoid Naming my own. I fear what I will discover when I feel the unbearable hurt inside "Little Andrea," the girl with the wayward hair. She still lives inside me, shrouded in regret and feeling inadequate. She needs me to come and help her find a way out of her misery.

We must stop ourselves from believing that a triggering experience that happened in childhood will not affect us, because deep wounds last a lifetime. When we discount the pain to make it go away, thinking we should be stronger, it only deepens the effects of the pain as well as what triggers us to run from it.

- What are the false identities within your core wounds and what pain can you Name?

- Do you have more than one shadow-version of yourself, and do they connect to a common pattern or theme?

- If you approached this younger version of yourself, what would you say or do to help, console, or salve the pain of this wound?

When we connect directly at the pain point and re-parent the child inside our shadow selves, we compassionately offer them what we need to feel seen, heard, and loved. We all have something that impacted us, and we can never gauge how the wounds of others might haunt and shape their life. Some of us suffer traumas that change us forever. Some of us have blissful childhoods but are wounded all the same. No matter what your core wound may be, you can guarantee that it influences who you are and how you behave. Although you may believe you have healed your wound, if you are still defaulting to behavior that matches up with your false identity (which is probably a lot of below the line masculine and feminine energy), chances are your wound still affects the way you navigate life's challenges. Over time, core wounding imprints the soul, fueling the way we perceive our wholeness, and locking in denser energies that must be released from bondage if we are to align with our essential selves and find our Gentle Warriors.

I wish I could tell you that healing our core wounds is an easy process. It is not. The recurring themes that we struggle to overcome will continue to knock at us throughout our lives. Learning to Name the themes that haunt us is about recognizing the shadow-version of our false identities that contain all of the parts we don't want to admit to having. Hidden at first in our unconscious, it is only through the effort to become self-aware that we recognize the darkest parts of our false selves. Naming the shadow-version of ourselves is a journey back to the essential self, and a willingness to acknowledge that we have been wounded by something from our past. When we Name the thing that hurt us, we liberate the thorn that triggers our pain and feelings of unworthiness. The thorn of our wounding can only be removed by Naming it, acknowledging its power over us. It is natural to want to look away, ignore and deny our torment as we convince ourselves that if we stuff our uncomfortable emotions deep down, they will go away. We have a deep fear of feeling pain, so we surround our suffering with armor that causes our wounds to become a dark enigma of stuck energy that blocks us from the truest parts of our power. We further separate ourselves from this core pain by developing coping mechanisms to control our mindset. We distract ourselves by achieving, diving into our careers, and focusing on "self-improvement" so we can repair the "unacceptable" and "broken" parts of ourselves. It's like treating an infection on the surface of a wound instead of addressing the true source of the abscess with antibiotics.

Rickson guarded his core wound around abandonment with the armor of a warring warrior on alert. His father had died of a sudden heart attack when Rickson was just three, leaving his mother to raise him and his infant sister. Although his mother tried her best to fill in the gaps, Rickson created a very masculine and idealized version of his father that he projected out into the world:

"I craved being around my friends' dads, fantasizing about the qualities my father must have possessed—protector, confident mentor, and hard-edged competitor." He shared, "I wanted my dad to be the tough guy who would keep me safe, but all I had to go on was what my mother shared about him, so I created all the masculine qualities I thought I would need to prove that I was manly, strong, and could take care of myself."

Denying his belief that he was whole, Rickson convinced himself he had something to prove to the world about his masculine strength and worth. When he felt threatened, Rickson had a tendency to take off-hand comments personally, becoming combative and not giving others the benefit of the doubt. He was defensive, territorial, and always had to be right. As we explored the depths of his core wound, Rickson saw that his fury masked a deeper fear that he was deficient and unlovable because he did not have a father. He disliked this shadow-version of himself because he couldn't control it and its power caused him to default to the wounded below the line masculine behaviors of alienating, overpowering, and blaming others.

Rickson needed to get aligned with both sides of his wholeness, masculine and feminine. So together, he and I began to create new beliefs about the man that he wanted to present to the world. When Rickson Named his pain, he was able to understand its source and offer the shadow-version of himself compassion instead of shame for growing up fatherless. He used the masculine and feminine chart to pull out above the line responses we hoped to call in and embody going forward: confidence, ownership, independence, compassion, humble innovator, and adventurous explorer. When Rickson embraced his feminine side, he welcomed in the generous, resourceful, nurturing, and authentic parts of himself that were an intrinsic part of his wholeness. "When I become a dad, those are the kinds of qualities I want to embody," he said, "I'd like to think my dad would have agreed."

Naming Our Feelings

You are not your feelings, yet most of us are afraid to Name uncomfortable emotions. Our emotions reveal the truths about what is most important, so why are we so reluctant to feel and Name them? We hear of practices like meditation and journal writing that are supposed to provide both solace and insight, yet many of us are terrified to "be still" or acknowledge that our uncomfortable emotions exist. However, our feelings are the barometer to our soul, giving us vital information and pointing us to where we need to look so we can make peace with the parts of ourselves that we believe are broken or lacking. Emotions of any sort, good or bad, are a gift because they bring us closer to the source of our essential selves and what we might need to do to achieve emotional balance. When we Name our suffering and look at the story that we have created about an emotion, a false identity, or core wounding from the past, we receive ourselves with both love and compassion. It's like detaching yourself from the situation and looking at it with fresh eyes.

A warring warrior is someone who has never allowed themselves the gift of Naming uncomfortable emotions. Their emotions are trapped inside the blocked energy of false identities and core wounding and their actions or reactions are stuck in a constant cycle of below the line, wounded responses.

Before I became a life coach, I was a warring warrior, yet (lucky for me) part of my training was to experience the coaching process from the client perspective. In a deeper conversation with a mentor coach about my father, a core wound within my heart fired a warning shot that triggered a wrath of fury that rose-up unexpectedly in one of our sessions. "Anger," my coach explained, "is a cover-up emotion. What's under there? What emotion is your outrage concealing, Andrea?"

I was terrified, knowing that this intuitive woman had spied, not only a false identity, but my long-concealed core wound of inadequacy. It felt like she had popped a festering ulcer within a false identity that I didn't want to Name. I grew silent and hot tears welled up in my eyes as I allowed myself to feel long ignored emotions, tenderizing the deep pain that I had never been brave enough to Name. My father had not loved me in the way I needed to be loved. I sensed that he too had been wounded, excusing his rejection and his inability to connect with me, by further discounting my own feelings of inadequacy. By Naming this long-concealed false identity and the emotion attached to it, I allowed myself to see and accept my wound and generously offer it the compassion and love that it needed to heal. I closed my eyes and embraced the little girl who so wanted her father's love by soothing her, seeing her, and accepting her as whole. Until this moment, I had been using the rage of a warring warrior as armor and had not healed the hurt under my armor. By finally putting a Name to my wound and feeling it, I discovered the genius within the shadow-version of myself; I did not need my father's love to be whole, I only needed my own.

"To empower others, we must share from our scars, not our wounds."

—UNKNOWN

Just as I had used the false identity of being dumb as a calling to enlighten emergent readers, I gave the pain of my wound a purpose by choosing to extract its genius so I could be a way shower to other brave seekers who wanted to live in their own integrity. Transformation is an alchemical process that takes commitment, time, and practice. It is in the courageous act of choosing to sit with the shadow-version of ourselves that we ignite the brightest light within our own inner magnificence. The awareness of catching ourselves before we lash out with a wounded response means that we have learned new tools, like introspection, meditation, and the power of saying NO, to salve our triggers and choose a softer way through them. Part of my healing was an intentional effort to pivot my mindset so I could begin to repair the relationship with my father. This meant that in my interactions with him, I would be showing up differently.

Everything in your life reflects a conscientious choice. If you want a different result, you must choose to take a different path. It is the only way to redirect your life and change the outcomes. When I chose to

Name my pain with acceptance and forgiveness instead of stoicism and anger, I welcomed in compassion for myself and everyone in my orbit. I showed up differently, and in doing so, I welcomed in new energy and raised myself to a higher vibrational frequency. With new awareness of my feelings and freedom from the identity of an inadequate daughter, I no longer looked at life from a distorted point of view. By receiving myself at a higher frequency, I shifted my mindset, creating space for more of my light and love to shine through. I broke the dirty wash and rinse cycle of my past and became more strategic in the exchanges that I had with my dad, intentionally neutralizing a chiding remark by boldly daring myself to be kind but also truthful. When I consciously opened my heart to him, he surprisingly followed my lead.

One afternoon when he jokingly criticized me for a reason I do not recall, I looked him straight in the eye and said honestly, "Dad when you say things like that to me, it hurts my feelings. It is not funny, in fact, it is a mean thing to say to anyone, especially the daughter you are supposed to love. It's time for me to leave."

There was a sudden shift in the room and as I got up to exit, I spied deep regret in my father's 91-year-old face. "Annie, I'm sorry. You know I love to tease you," he jokingly countered.

"Saying unkind things does not feel like love to me, Dad, it only tears a hole in my heart. I think there are people out there that would be honored to have a daughter like me. I wish you were nicer to me."

I had spoken my truth, but I also regretted the hot tears that welled up in my eyes. I was finally showing him my divine feminine side. My father looked at me with anguish and in that small moment, I knew that he had seen and heard the voice of a very different woman.

"I am sorry, Annie," he said earnestly. "Please come over here and give me a hug. I am sorry I hurt you."

Although I wanted to resist meeting him where he was, I caught myself, seeing that old age had softened him. I needed to allow him to offer up the best of himself.

> "I used to be afraid of the dark until I learned
> that I am light and the dark is afraid of me."
>
> —D.R. SILVA

We all have a sword of regret that needs to be surrendered. True healing is an intentional choice and only happens when you decide to see your pain by Naming it. I did not want to carry any regret or anger towards my father anymore, and although our relationship is by no means perfect, it is so much more that I had ever hoped that it could be. When I started writing as a way to Name emotion, I even got vulnerable by writing a story that honored him. It was about a favorite day that he and I had spent skiing together. In the piece, I told my dad all the things that I dare not say out loud. When I gave him the story to read, he cried and told me he loved not only the storytelling but remembering our special day together. Why wait until someone is gone to tell them you love them, faults and all?

After her alcoholic mother died, Kelsey took two years to find a way to come to terms with the pain she had endured in her very dysfunctional childhood. After her mother's remains were cremated, Kelsey tucked the ashes discreetly to the back of a closet, unsure of how to process her mother's death. Kelsey wrote her mother a letter naming all of the feelings she had never said out loud. Writing the letter to her mother helped Kelsey see and Name the pain of a long unattended wound and begin to heal it. Kelsey then decided it was time for closure, and she and her siblings gathered and celebrated her mother's life, scattering the ashes from a mountaintop along with the charred remains of the letter Kelsey had written to her mother.

"It was amazingly cathartic," she shared, "but something kind of spooky happened too." Kelsey explained that as their group turned to walk back down the trail, a red tail hawk circled just above, flashing its auburn tail feathers proudly. "I am choosing to take that as a sign that my mom got the letter." she laughed.

Put very simply, Naming our wounds enhances our relationship with our essential self, not just our radiant parts, but the darker bits hidden within our shadow-version. We must heal ourselves from the inside out, the counterintuitive process of Naming our pain so we can understand it. When we conscientiously Name the wound and label the false identities we have used to camouflage it, we release the trapped energy of our emotion by offering compassion, mercy and tenderness to the injured parts of ourselves that lie deep inside our core wounds. Instead of seeing ourselves as broken, flawed, and inadequate, we emerge with a better understanding of how the shadow-version of ourselves has made us more resilient: *I am unique, interesting, and whole.* If we are lucky, we end the patterns for our children by not doing what our parents might have done: minimize, ignore, discount. When I finally let go of the external circumstances I had for my father's approval, I began to see the radiant light I was meant to offer the world. I also paid it forward and forged a new relationship with my father that reflected a more authentic version of the woman I had become: "I love you, Dad" I tell him each time we part, and my father answers back, "I love you too, Sweetie."

There is both hope and wisdom under our wounds—false identities and the emotions inside them. It's never too late in life to reconcile a core wounding and update a false identity. When we Name them, they will lead us to the next step in the framework of living a well-lived life, Claim. Boldly Name the shadow-versions of yourself so you can then Claim the second essential step in the way of the Gentle Warrior.

CHAPTER FOUR

Claim

After we have named our false identities, core wounds and the emotional behaviors they trigger, we are ready to Claim new behavior, new energy, and enter cleaner relationships with ourselves and others. When we Claim, we take responsibility for our past patterns by identifying them and making the decision to no longer engage with ourselves, and others, in the ways we have in the past. We are retraining ourselves to notice when old patterns show up so we can pivot into a new state of awareness. We are proactive instead of reactive.

While we may not be able to control when we are triggered by our inner critic, the energies of the outside world (and all the personalities within it), and our fundamental relationships, we can Claim what we do with the emotion in the moment. The internal chatter of our inner critic, the outside energy in our society, and the fluidity in our relationships can be countered by the new awareness of our default to a below the line, or wounded response. Claiming is solidifying the person you can become by dancing curiously between the masculine and feminine nuances within yourself.

Which traits do you want to highlight, and which ones do you need to cast aside? In this simple act itself, we are boldly Claiming a new mindset or new way of being. To Claim takes courage and a willingness to accept that as we make the decision to transform, we must also become more perceptive about what triggers doubt, resentment, and fear, or the looping pattern caused by the past false identities and core wounds. When we choose curiosity, we buy into the playfulness that comes with exploration. With clients, it is in their willingness to get curious about the unknown beliefs of the shadow-versions they have created for themselves that begins to shed light on the fears of the inner critic and their past defaults to a below the line/wounded response. Just the thought of entering the unknown of a dark cave sounds terrifying, so we grab a figurative lantern and enter together: "What is it like in here?" "What color do you see?" "What is your greatest fear here?"

This step is where I witness fierce bravery in my clients. Our ability to explore and understand the why behind the shadow-versions of themselves relies solely on their willingness to Name and face these fears. You can't be curious and afraid at the same time. Nine months into COVID-19 isolation, Lauren Named that she worried that her insecure and needy, below the line responses meant that she might have borderline depression tendencies because she hated to be alone.

"The isolation has been torture for me and I dread my empty apartment. I also worry that my friends will accuse me of being clingy and too co-dependent if I reach out to meet-up," she confided.

"It seems like you have a lot of judgement around your feelings of loneliness," I offered. "Would you be willing to explore the feelings you encounter in your empty apartment so you can Name the why of it and then Claim an above the line action?"

Intrigued with the possibility of Claiming new energy, Lauren bravely entered the cave of her loneliness and discovered that her inner critic was most afraid of her inability to "handle being alone." As we ventured further into the shadow-version she held for herself, I asked her: "What does your loneliness need now?"

"Human connection, I miss being around people," she said. "I need to reach out to others, so I feel like I am part of something more than just myself and this empty apartment. Too much isolation for me means melancholy."

An extrovert who thrived on human interaction, Lauren found the antidote to her loneliness inside of her shadow-version of self. "No wonder you're lonely, Lauren, you are a social being and recharge your energy by being around people. What action will you Claim to take control?" I asked her.

Instead of judging herself as being an overly emotional person who couldn't be alone, Lauren gained insight to her emotions and Claimed an action or antidote (reaching out to others) to counteract her secret fear of being depressed. The genius within the shadow-version of herself had revealed that in order for Lauren to feel balanced, she needed to be intentional about integrating human interaction into her life. Lauren's action plan included not only reaching out for support from others when she was feeling isolated, but also sprucing up specific areas of her apartment for working-out, meditating, and socializing. By consciously receiving herself in whatever emotion she was feeling, Lauren began to accept that her shadow-version of self was as important to her well-being as her people person side.

"When my shadow shows up it is a sign that I need to check in with myself," she said.

There is self-compassion when we allow ourselves to understand the why behind our fears, and depending on the trigger, a backlash if we are not courageous enough to Claim a new response. It's like a child learning to walk, some of the steps you take will land firmly, while others, minor stumbles, will provide important information about the new identities emerging within you that may need more practice and refinement.

Like adopting any new practice, repetition and observation builds the muscles we need to make what is at first unfamiliar a standard practice. When we replace fear with curiosity, and receive ourselves in kindness, it is much easier to laugh off the bloopers that we will most certainly encounter. Imagine what we can do on this earth if we could begin to dissolve the hidden secrets, fears, and emotions that keep us from stepping into our essential selves. It is what fuels the vision of who we are and how we support each other. We must Claim ourselves inside first, the slow and steady process of becoming an observer in your own life.

Elle came to coaching, in her words, "to create more presence and harmony" in her life. Elle was wound tightly and in our first session together, she struggled to conjure even one memory of a time in her life when she had felt calm and at peace. Elle was so focused on achievement, that she never allowed herself to detach from it. Emotionally exhausted, her life had morphed into an ego driven strive for perfection that had her up in the wee hours of the morning, second guessing yesterday's achievements. Elle's feminine traits of accountability and responsiveness were harassed incessantly by an arrogant and controlling masculine energy that never allowed her a moment of peace, let alone the idea of any form of decant relaxation. Constantly at war with herself, Elle felt like she was existing rather than living. She felt like a worn-down pencil that had to work hard to stay sharp.

"What are you most afraid of?" I asked her.

"Failure, appearing lazy and being judged by others," she answered resolutely.

In guiding Elle to Name her fear of failure and judgment, a wound fueled by what she called, "The Rodecker Ambition" or her father's high expectations of her, Elle began the first step to naming her exhaustion from trying to outrun her fear, and Claim the action needed to change her mindset so she could create more balance between her life and work.

One of the first steps I take with clients is teaching them to Claim their internal triggers by noticing when that shaming or critical voice, or the inner critic (Kimsey-House, Kimsey-House, Sandahl and Whitworth, 2011) shows up in their thinking. Claiming the chatter of an inner critic helps clients to isolate the voice that questions their thinking and keeps them from trusting their gut. Learning to notice your inner critic's voice is a very powerful first step in the Claiming process because it begins to weaken the patterns of the dirty wash and rise cycle I spoke of in Chapter Three. You get ahead of your old default tendency to react by noticing when triggered emotions and self-limiting thoughts arrive, choosing instead to break old patterns of the past so you can Claim responses that better match the vision of who you are becoming.

The Co-Active Institute, where I did my coach training, defines the dissonate voice inside your head as your saboteur; or inner critic: "The voice is there to keep you from taking unsafe risks, but it is overcautious at a time that calls for risks the sake of change and (living) a more fulfilling life."*

Think of your inner critic as your anti-superpower the voice of perfectionism that arrives to remind you of your inadequacy or simply, the self-limiting voice of reason that keeps you from stepping into your truest potential. Sometimes, like Elle's "Rodecker Ambition," an inner critic's voice can be inspired by critical people in our life. Maybe a cynical parent, a hard driving coach, or a skeptical boss. No matter who inspires the voice, when it shows up, it causes you to doubt yourself and argues that you should "play" only within your comfort zone. In truth, the inner critic voice is an expression of the safety instinct that we have

---

* *Kimsey-House, Kimsey-House, Sandahl and Whitworth Co-Active Coaching*, Changing Business Transforming Lives, Third Edition (2011)

within us. Your inner critic wants to save you from any kind of emotional risk—hurt, failure, criticism, disappointment, or rejection. When we begin to understand that our inner critic voice stems from old fears that might be inspired from childhood or a traumatic experience from the past, it becomes easier to run interference, shift your thinking, and Claim a new outcome. When you understand that the inner critic's main objective is to keep you safe, you'll notice its attempts to bully, judge, and criticize you anytime you step out of your safety zone. Inner critics tend to scream loudest at new beginnings, just as you are stepping into your power. Once you begin to gain awareness of their hall monitor ways, you start to catch them before they creep in and foil your plans, dreams, and aspirations (Kimsey-House, Kimsey-House, Sandahl and Whitworth, 2011) (Mohr, 2015).

Make a list of when your inner critic shows up in your thinking throughout the day. Write down every thought that stings or makes you take a pause. Think, "I am not this voice." Focus in on what false identities or past experiences might be causing you to doubt yourself. Remember, your inner critic is trying to keep you from failure, rejection, and embarrassment.

Your inner critic might say things like, "Why are you being lazy and sleeping in?" "You aren't ready for that promotion, you are too scattered." "You aren't good at that!" or "What if you fail, you'll look stupid!"

A big piece of Claiming is to separate ourselves from the below the line emotions this inner critic voice triggers by noticing that we have been hooked or stung by something or someone that has fueled the power of the inner critic, or "the committee in our head." While sometimes awareness of this self-doubting voice can be enough, with most clients I take it one step further by helping them to Claim the voice by creating a character who personifies the emotion so they can understand its motives and how it might be attempting to keep them safe. Unlike the story of Lauren who had awareness around how to separate herself from her inner critic's chatter, Elle was so intertwined and codependent with her inner critic, that she needed a new gimmick to weaken its hold on her mindset. Together we created a character, "Vanessa," who reminded Elle of a rather vindictive roommate she had in college. Vanessa embodied the nagging voice of Elle's slave-driving trigger because, as Elle explained, "She was competitive, judgmental, and never gave me credit for anything. No matter how hard I tried, Vanessa always made me feel incompetent and substandard."

"What do you think Vanessa is most worried about?" I asked her, trying to further separate Elle from the voice in her head.

"She's afraid that I haven't done enough and that I'll be seen by others as lazy," said Elle earnestly.

"If Vanesa is still in college, do you think she has current information about you, your job and how hard you work?" I continued.

"No, Vanessa has no idea at all."

"So, if you encountered Vanessa now, what might you tell her to calm her fears about you appearing lazy and unprepared?"

"I'd tell her to **** off," Elle laughed.

"True, but what if we realize that Vanessa is really trying to keep you safe. What could you say to Vanessa to reassure her that you've got things covered?"

There always a 1% truth in the concerns of your inner critic because the voice is sincerely motivated to keep you safe from harm. Your inner critic is like a doting parent who reminds you to wear a sweater in 80-degree weather. What you really want to say to them is "thanks for the reminder, Mom, but I know what is best for me." Elle's Vanessa, although judgmental and driven, was genuinely protecting Elle from failure and embarrassment. The inner critic's catty speeches had become so influential and part of Elle's subconsciousness, that she didn't trust her gut instinct anymore. Instead of allowing Vanessa's chatter to fill in the gaps, Elle needed to begin using her own voice to take up more space in her thinking. This is where we can use above the line masculine and feminine strategies to kindly reason with the voice and then send it away. Elle began to use this kind of dialog when Vanessa arrived on the scene:

"Hi Vanessa, I understand that you are worried about me looking lazy, but I've got us covered and am very prepared for tomorrow's meeting. I will be much better equipped if I get a good night's sleep, so I am asking you to please leave me alone."

As silly as this conversation might sound, it is tangible and allows the client to intentionally take their power back. When I am coaching and sense that a client's inner critic might be in our session, I might say something like, "Wait, it sounds like your inner critic is in the room with us, can you please open the door and ask it to leave?"

These kinds of somatic tools get the client out of their head and into their heart by calling in a playful humor and allowing clients to see how internal chatter may have kept them from trusting their gut instincts. By directly calling out the voice, we diminish its power, detach from its self-limiting beliefs, and call in a bit of levity in the heat of a tense moment.

So, what does "somatic" mean? Simply put, it means "body." We are detaching from the chatter of our minds by inviting our body to a new setting (like a visualization) and adding a bit of humor into the conversation. Somatic tools support presence, which is a prerequisite for being in a relationship with anything. Embodied awareness, or presence, helps clients engage with their life in a more connected way. Somatic tools like Lauren's exploration of the dark cave of her shadow-self or the character that Elle created for her inner critic, help clients Claim the full spectrum of their emotions. We bring their feelings into the light to understand them and their source. When we

Claim a new way to be with difficult emotions, such as fear, sadness, grief, and anger, it also empowers us to be with pleasurable emotions, such as joy and love, and the pleasurable states of abundance and peace. All of these can be held with loving awareness when we have more somatic capacity.

How to Claim and Tame
of Your Inner Critic

1.   The first step is to gain awareness by becoming an observer in your own life. *When do you notice the voice showing up in your thinking?*

- At the start of a new experience or situation?

- When you begin to take up more space or step into your power?

- Is it related to a false identity or limiting belief?

2.   Catch yourself when you're feeling anxious, angry, or convinced you will fail. Try to separate yourself from the chatter of the voice and get curious:

- What does it say?

- What is it trying to keep you safe from?

- What situations trigger the voice? (Look for patterns and themes that match a core wound or false identity of the past).

- What might be the root of the fear or limiting belief? (Family members, old teachers, cultural messages).

3.   How relevant and up to date are your inner critic's fears? What do you know about the situation that might ease its worry and doubt?

(Remember, your inner critic's job is help you to feel safe and in control.) *Ask yourself:*

- What am I afraid of?

- What would it mean if that happened?

- Is this a realistic fear?

- How can I update this self-limiting belief with more current information?

4. Allow yourself space to dig deeper and Name your most vulnerable feelings about the situation. Your inner critic is protecting you from naming your fear so you will be safe from Claiming your power. Do you really need all that protection? Probably not. A Gentle Warrior can handle it!

5. Create a character that personifies the voice so you can call it out when it shows up. Thank your inner critic for its concerns, update it with the current facts and assure the voice that you've got things covered going forward. "I understand you are worried about _____ but I've got us covered so you need not worry. Please leave me alone I can get back to more important things."

Besides helping separate ourselves from the self-limiting thinking of the inner critic, using somatic tools helps us get comfortable Claiming new behaviors that can replace our past default to below the line, wounded responses. When Elle began to notice and Claim her emotions, she took control and began to allow herself, not only more moments of presence, but a calmer state of mind that included more restful nights. It wasn't that Vanessa never showed up, but when she did, Elle recognized her presence and learned to Name the issue and Claim more peace and harmony in her work-life balance. In one of our sessions together, Elle shared that she had bought a journal so she could intentionally savor experiences when she felt present, like a beautiful sunset or a generous compliment that she wanted to soak in and cherish a bit longer. The practice slowed her down so Elle could counteract her past patterns and Vanessa's catty comments.

Elle also began to explore how both her masculine and feminine sides impacted her ability to achieve presence. She curated a list of above the line qualities that she hoped to embody while also Claiming the wounded, below the line triggers that she wanted to curb and gain more awareness of. She discovered when she leaned too much into her above the line feminine strengths of efficiency and organization, she ran the risk of converting these positive characteristics into the rather nasty, masculine below the line trait of, "being controlling."

"I understand now that my past tendencies to control outcomes bordered on aggressive because they were based in fear. When I catch myself, talk to my fear and understand what has caused it, I Claim it and choose an above the line trait that will serve me and how I want to show up in the world."

We are making the choice to evolve into a more awakened version of ourselves when we Claim the trigger as the source of our emotion, and shift the energy into the productive attributes of our above the line masculine and feminine behaviors. Claiming is acknowledging the emotion's power over us so we can create an action that aligns more with our integrity. Quite simply, naming and Claiming gives us mastery over past triggers, opening us wide to "the good, the bad, and the ugly" of the shadow-version of ourselves. It is only when we receive ourselves and our pain that we find a tangible way to change our responses to it.

Claiming Your Unique Energy

Your energy, the combination of gifts and light that you bring to the world, introduces you before you utter a word. Like an electrical current, people feel your energetic vibration and either like it or dislike it. While this all sounds a bit groovy, think of the impact of your energy as the unique calling card of emotion that you unconsciously release when you enter a room. While some leave a scent of joyful and expansive vibes, others attack us in a fog of constrictive energy that we have a hard time shaking off. Have you ever met someone whose energy is so faint that you hardly feel their presence? The impact we make on one another comes down to the energy vibrations that we give off and take in.

An energy collision is when you feel the effects of someone's energy and wonder why it impacted you in either a positive or negative way. You walk away either inspired or extremely drained. Some people have such strong energy that it can instantly change the dynamics of a situation. We have all been on a Zoom call where someone's energy takes up so much space that we feel pushed aside, crowded out or invisible. There are also charismatic people that have such dynamic energy that we all want to stop, look, and listen. Energy is important and once you are clear on how to align and replenish you own energy, being aware of the energy around you will help you anticipate and navigate potential energy draining situations.

When we are not aligned with our essential selves, it throws both our internal and external energies out of whack. Claiming and realigning your own unique energy is critical before we can expect to sift and sort the varied energy vibrations of those who cross in and out of our orbit. While the recalibration of who we are and how we show up can be extremely satisfying and fulfilling, it's not surprising that as you evolve and change, you will encounter both conflict and confusion in your interpersonal encounters. When you Claim a new way of being, not everyone is going to like it. As you gain more awareness of the kind of energy you hope to attract within yourself, you may discover that certain energies of the past, do not match the energy you hope to welcome into the future.

Being around negative or toxic energy affects the way we see ourselves, and awareness around energy boundaries is another essential tool that I present to clients. Before we can center ourselves in our own energy, it is important to learn how to shield ourselves from "other people's energy." Many things in life can zap our energy—travel, Zoom calls, commuting, noisy public spaces, a cranky toddler, or a cranky grandpa. But the most toxic energy zappers are "energy vampires" who prey on your kindness and literally suck your energy dry. They are the people who boost their own energy by taking energy from others via an argument, criticism, belittlement or just a very one-sided conversation.

While not everyone qualifies as an energy vampire, some people just project more negative energy out into the world. You might have someone in your life who brags about accomplishments and downplays the contributions of others. Maybe you know a drama queen who takes up unreasonable amounts of your time and overshares. No matter who the energy zapper is, as we expand our awareness and begin to Claim more of our power, the frequency of the energy we are putting out pulls us forward, forcing us to recalibrate our energy and upgrade our surroundings.

Mia, a soft-spoken graphic designer, landed an entry level position at a small company. Underestimating her talents as a vital member of the team, Mia delighted in learning all aspects of the business and soon became a well versed "jack of all trades." After three years, however, Mia began to have growing pains. She wanted to explore her options in the field and approached her boss for candid career advice, "Each time I met with him, sharing what I hoped for the future, he dodged my questions, undercut my skill set and made inferences that he would offer me more experience under his mentorship."

Mia trusted him, after all, he had bet on her when she was an inexperienced and eager college student. Yet, as time passed with no hope of advancement, Mia quietly began to search for new opportunities. She found a bigger job with a competitor and when she respectfully gave her two weeks' notice, her boss became enraged, accusing her of being disloyal and manipulative. "I was so surprised at his reaction," she said. "I thought he'd be happy for me, but he took my departure as a personal attack. I realized that I was no longer the meek employee that he had hired. The more confident and skilled I became, the more he tried to hold me back."

You have no obligation to rebuild a relationship with someone who has hurt you, and just because you have forgiven them and moved on from the experience, doesn't mean that they did not have toxic energy. Mia now saw that her mentor had always been an energy vampire, domineering, self-centered and unsupportive. His reactive anger was clearly more about his loss, not her gain. "It's a backhanded compliment, I suppose. He is going to miss me, and I realize now that our relationship was toxic and unbalanced from the very start."

Claiming a new energy upgrade for herself helped Mia gain insight into her past experiences when she had defaulted to more submissive below the line responses, not only in her career but in her interpersonal relationships.

"I not only mourn for my younger self, but I am angry that I allowed others to undercut my power and take advantage of my demur kindness. It has happened all my life and now it is time for me Claim myself first."

Mia Named that her past patterns of complacency, codependence and victimhood came from giving others undue authority long after they were worthy. Although she regretted the pain of this shadow-version of herself, the experience was the tipping point that compelled her to finally Claim ownership of the talents and aspirations of the woman she had become.

When we Claim, we begin to practice self-sovereignty, or being the exclusive authority over the state of our own body and mind. Achieving self-sovereignty means learning to build an intentional architecture to support the boundaries of your internal energy force. This practice is essential to maintain a healthy level of reserve, especially when we encounter life's challenges.

When Phoebe was diagnosed with Stage-3 breast cancer, she came to coaching to Claim a new energy mindset so she could explore the concept of vulnerability and the notion of surrendering to the circumstances the universe had presented her.

"I want to develop a deeper understanding of myself that will lead me to where the 'juice' is," she explained. "I don't want cancer to define me, I want to flip the paradigm so I can find the gifts within it."

Phoebe's courage inspired me, the idea of building a structure that could shift her thought frequency and help her to transition into this challenge with both purpose and vision. Phoebe was Claiming the inner resources of herself. As Phoebe and I began our work together, we unraveled a theme many women struggle to overcome, our default to control outcomes. Control is a fear-based and wounded masculine response that constricts our ability to receive both the offerings of others and the genius or wisdom inside adverse situations. She and I had in depth conversations on how to implement the act of surrendering to her daily life by "accepting what is, instead of what is not." In Phoebe's struggle to relinquish control, I saw my own and leaned into the inspired wisdom she was offering.

Before cancer, Phoebe had been the picture of perfection. She was the thoughtful good neighbor who delivered home cooked meals to your doorstep or the dear friend who volunteered to take your children overnight. Now, after her cancer diagnosis, Phoebe's life felt unruly, messy, and imperfect. As she gained awareness of the need to manage the new vulnerabilities that she was feeling, Phoebe began to Claim new norms for her energy boundaries.

When Parents' Weekend arrived at her daughter's university, Phoebe was a few treatments into her chemotherapy. Her hair, one week away from disintegrating, was brittle and secured in a very fragile ponytail. As she prepared for her trip, Phoebe wanted to protect the fringes of herself, and worried that well intended fellow parents might notice her fragile appearance and offer unwanted sympathy. All Phoebe wanted was to harvest the presence and joy of visiting her college co-ed, "This weekend is about our daughter, and I don't want anyone to pop our joy bubble." she said adamantly, "I want to create a graceful boundary that will protect the confines of my vulnerability now."

Because Phoebe had limited energy and was not yet ready to share her illness with a larger community, together we created a structure of practices that would serve her throughout her treatment and beyond it. Instead of addressing well intended comments that weekend, she smiled politely, redirecting the conversation to the excitement of Parents' Weekend. This was a new frequency for Phoebe, who before cancer, had been the social center of everything. Yet now she needed to make an intentional effort to store her energy reserves within the boundaries for herself.

Phoebe wanted to become more conscious when the edges of her comfort zone had been violated. This meant that she needed to shift her concept of "doing for others," an above the line feminine strength, and call-in a more introspective and self-compassionate focus by "being available for herself." She developed new rituals that would feed her energy; natural remedies to combat nausea and a short list of close friends who accompanied her to treatments. She also got more comfortable with vulnerability, curious about the genius within it and what it might teach her about courage. Instead of resisting it, she allowed herself to receive support and show weakness. She learned a new portal for inner strength and in doing so, she embraced the grace of receiving. In redefining herself and what she needed from the inside out, Phoebe attuned with the rich resources available within the boundaries of her own precious energy reserve. When we Claim the sovereignty of ourselves, we find the path to the Gentle Warrior within.

Creating Energetic Boundaries

Each time you go out into the world, you encounter "other people's energy." Like breathing in the fresh air of a spring afternoon or avoiding a puff of secondhand smoke, Claiming a more balanced state of energy flow requires noticing both the incoming and outgoing influences around you. While most of us cannot retreat when life starts to pull at us, it is important to learn how to shield ourselves from the toxins of life so we can go towards the things that speak to our soul. Just like a first responder who stabilizes the frantic energy of a crisis with calm, confident energy, you have the power to Claim a better frequency of energy for yourself and everyone in your orbit.

Many of us don't have a strong awareness of the power of energy, never mind how to maintain a healthy balance to our own energy frequencies. Yet, when our energy reserves get depleted we default to below the line, reactive behaviors that cause us to feel disconnected to our essential selves.

So how do we create energetic boundaries with above the line behavior despite how people in our environment are acting? We have to let go of our attachment to a specific expectation of how we want a person to act and treat us. We set ourselves up for disappointment if that expectation is not met, and we become frustrated or angry. That person may not be behaving as we like, but we are giving our power away by allowing their behavior to affect us. If the person treats us nicely, we feel happy, but if it's the opposite and the person is unkind, we feel hurt and think, "I'm not getting the love that I deserve. I'm not being accepted!"

Although, it is natural to want to be liked and accepted by others, when we become attached to an outcome by trying to win someone over, we give our precious energy away instead of creating a boundary to protect it. The first step in creating an energy boundary is to notice and release the attachment to the other person. If, for example, someone is treating you disrespectfully, release the notion of expecting them to be any other way than how they are behaving. Respect yourself and migrate towards people who do show you respect. When we power our own energy by expecting that the person who is misbehaving will make us feel better, we are triggered by their pain and the negative energy around it.

Try the "not my circus, not my monkeys" approach by detaching from their energy with something like, "Yikes, that person was super negative, but that is their thing. I'm energetically removing myself because their stuff is not my stuff. I don't need that person to make me feel good about myself. I'm taking full responsibility for myself and Claiming my own energy."

You have just created an energetic boundary. Take it one step further by using a somatic tool, stretch out your hands in front of you to block their energy: "This is my energy boundary and the space beyond my hands is the other person's responsibility, not mine."

You may even need to step back or ask the person to not come any closer—it's your right to guard your energy boundaries. Although taking ownership of your own space may not change the other person's behavior, it is the first step in releasing your attachment so you can Claim and root into our own unique energy. Creating an energetic boundary is the graceful practice of self-sovereignty. When we take full ownership for the space we need to be grounded in our energy, we set a clear intention for ourselves and those in our orbit.

Obviously, there are times when we encounter emotional confusion or drama that will trigger us deeply, where it is challenging to think about creating energetic boundaries. When we take on another's heavy emotion, it is even more imperative that we connect to our heart so we can Name what we are feeling and Claim what we want to do about the energy of the emotion that we are interacting with. It is the simple act of becoming present with your own energy frequency:

- **NAME**: What is my emotional need at this moment?
- **CLAIM**: What do I want to do feel safe and grounded in my own energy?

But sometimes, especially with those close to us, it not that easy and we get lost in the drama, the emotion, or the reactivity of the situation. This is when it is essential that we step back and ask ourselves: "What is my goal in this situation?"

- I want to have a clear and positive state of mind.
- I want to be productive and grounded in my energy.

- I want to be aligned with myself so I can offer kindness to the people around me.

We check in with ourselves, not to change the behavior of another person, but to get in harmony with ourselves. Claiming self-sovereignty is taking care of your emotional state of mind first and foremost. Although the goal of the emotional person might be to unload negativity and to vent anger, your intention might be to have a positive outcome that will serve your energy frequency. When I talk to someone who is being excessively negative, initially I try to be empathetic. However, if the trajectory of the exchange continues, I think to myself, "I don't want to be around this negative energy anymore," and I politely end the conversation. I am Claiming the intention of protecting myself from incoming energy that is not good for me. A big part of Claiming is the intentional act of self-sovereignty.

Once you have a clear intention of where you are going, it is much more manageable to create an energetic boundary and Claim your own energy. Let's say you are being triggered by a colleague at work. Separate yourself by grounding in your own energy and then Claim your intention by designing objectives like these examples:

- My intention is to have a positive state of mind for myself at work.
- I want to ground my own inner resourcefulness.

The "why" behind this reasoning might be:

- Because I want to have a good day where I'm happy and feel productive.
- I don't want to deplete my energy reserves by engaging in below the line behaviors of victimhood, blame, hate, or engaging in drama.

- I want to nourish habits that support my personal growth, and slowly cast off my wounded behaviors of the past.

When you set a clear intention for who you want to be when you encounter conflict, your plan of action might look like this:

- If this happens again with my coworker, I'm going to connect with myself and create a boundary.
- I'm going to be kind to the person even if they are being mean.
- I'm going to politely create an energetic boundary by ending the conversation.
- I'm going to say that I've got things to do, walk away, and wish them a good day.
- "Not my circus, not my monkeys."

Claiming by setting a clear intention for your internal energy helps you to navigate not only negative conflicts but practicing the art of energy alignment. We are only as good as our inside energy reserves, and they determine the way we show up on the outside. People who have learned how to Claim their own energy understand how critical it is to control what they are exposed to, and through a patient practice of trial and error, have adopted strategies to regulate the forces in their life that deplete them.

Maintaining healthy energy boundaries is a constant dance that requires grace, grit, and a sense of humor. First, Naming how you are triggered and then Claiming what you are going to "do" about it. We need to give ourselves permission to try and fail and then try again. Somedays I am so aligned with my internal energy that I embody Tara Brach, the much-admired meditation teacher. Other days, I am triggered and wound so tightly that the thought of Naming and Claiming my own energy feels more like being chained to something I don't want to see or feel.

What I can share, is that those of you who avoid grounding in your own energy have the most to gain. Your essential self, your Gentle Warrior, is calling to you to notice and center yourself in the resources of your own self-sovereignty. There is an intelligence, wisdom and clarity that can only be accessed when we are still and grounded. The dirty little secret is that "stillness" does not have to be still to be effective. You can find stillness in the garden, on a walk around your neighborhood, or by dancing in your car. Anything will work, the only requirement is to get out of your head and into your heart.

Relationships

To stand solidly in the Claim stage involves a mourning period of letting go of who you were when you allowed others to treat you a certain way, and the past patterns that were once connected to your core wounds and their false identities. As you step into a higher frequency of energy, there will be people from the past that no longer fit the story you are writing for the future. When you start to Name and Claim at a higher frequency of energy, no matter where you are at in your life, you will be choosing again: new people, new interests, and a new way of living. It is a big shift that may impact career choices, love interests, and friendships. You are suddenly discovering that some of your past relationship attractions were fueled by core wounds and their false identities.

With careers and families, women are tasked with navigating a smorgasbord of interpersonal exchanges. When our children are school aged, we have the opportunity and the curse of being exposed to a wide variety of unique personalities. If we are lucky, we reap the rewards of this period of life by collecting a cherished cluster of comrades we can raise our children beside. However, there is another side to raising school aged children—dealing with the fellow parents that irritate, annoy, and bring out the worst in us. I remember the women I knew who would "drink and email," writing an angry or vindictive response and hitting reply all. Your most logical answers are most definitely not at the bottom of a chardonnay bottle. Throughout our life, we have been navigating the energy variants of high school, college, work friendships, and whatever philanthropic endeavors tug at our hearts.

Changes to intimate relationships are the first sign that we may be expanding our thinking and moving in a different direction. Dissonant experiences often serve as the catalyst we need to Claim the future we are choosing. Just out of graduate school, my college boyfriend had shredded my confidence and inhibited my ability stand in the radiance of who I was becoming, both personally and professionally. After licking the wounds of our breakup, I intentionally upgraded my benchmark for all future romantic alliances. I Claimed that I wanted more (a lot more) than the fun-loving frat boy archetype of my college days. Part of Claiming this upgrade was to redefine myself as a woman who did not need a man to complete her. Although I dated, I guarded my heart and secretly kept a list of the traits that I required in a lifelong partner. I also enjoyed being single. You really do have to kiss a lot of toads to find your handsome prince. When I met my husband, who called me when he was going to be late, could fix anything, and respectfully opened doors for me, I thought, "This is a man, not a boy. I deserve this, a mature relationship based on mutual respect."

After hearing of my engagement through mutual friends, my college boyfriend called me in the wee hours of the morning, drunk and professing his love. With clarity on the contrast between who I had been and the updated mindset of who I had become, I offered him a kind but resolute reply, "I am sorry." I told him, "You will always be my first love, but we are through. I am in love with some else now. I wish you a very happy life."

As I hung up the phone, I quietly thanked my college boyfriend for all the lessons he had taught me about love. Without the wounds of this first love, I would never have been ready for the upgraded energy frequency of Bill DeWitt.

Whether it is intentional or happens gradually over the course of decades, when you transform, be ready to stand in the new energy of your upgrade. The first Christmas I was married, my parents struggled with the "in-law" factor. Bill and I needed to break new ground in the form of creating a sacred boundary for our household of two. When I announced that our Christmas morning would not include a visit home, my mother was very disappointed and told me so. The false identity of "being a good daughter" tugged at my values around family loyalty, and my mother's brooding about how this changed her life did not help matters. However, with the help of my new husband, I stood my ground. Energy expansion upsets those in our orbit and we must get comfortable taking up more space as we begin to tune into the new frequency of who we are becoming.

My daughter, who had always been known as "Katie," boldly chose to change her Name to "Kate" when she landed the job of her dreams. She Claimed this new upgraded version of herself by changing her personal email address, her LinkedIn profile and politely requesting that everyone refer to her ever after as, Kate.

"Katie is the cute little girl who quietly sat in the corner and waited for someone to tell her what to do," she explained. "I am ready to be the adult in the room and take charge of my life decisions going forward."

Hearing "Kate" took getting used to, but she was Claiming a new identity and a new way of being closer to the more authentic spirit of her Gentle Warrior within. Although her young life is still unfolding, Kate's relationship with herself has changed and will no doubt affect everything from her social calendar to her choices of the heart.

As women, we all struggle to find our authentic voice as we navigate a life and work balance, our changing bodies as we age, keeping our marriages fresh, and staying relevant in our careers. There are awakenings and setbacks that push at our energetic boundaries. Maybe you experience financial struggle, get divorced or move to a new town and need to rally alliances you can trust. Who are our true friends when we are going through a rough patch? Some of us don't understand the answer to this question until we awaken in a new stage during a crisis or a life transition. No matter what your age or stage, there will be setbacks and a need to sort and shift your energy boundaries.

The relationships you had in your twenties will no doubt differ greatly from the relationships you choose in your fifties. You have evolved and are looking for deeper connections that match where you are headed. When my youngest child graduated from high school, a quiet relief settled over me as I gratefully released all the individuals from my orbit that I no longer had to interact with, ever again. Admit it, we aren't attracted to everyone, yet we make nice and tolerate the people we encounter for the greater good and to set an example for our children. Although there are moments, I wish I could take back (like the time I was kind of snippy to the entitled woman in our neighborhood carpool who never drove her ride-share shift), for the most part I learned how to get along, who I could trust, and who I needed to avoid. I now celebrate this energetic shedding as one of the blessings of my middle age and stage. You can shed people at any time, which I highly recommend if you choose to Claim a self-sovereignty that is closer to your Gentle Warrior.

The ebb and flow of relationships teaches us the hard way who we can Claim as trustworthy, and who we need to "breakup" with. Years ago, in my mid-thirties, I befriended a woman named Carol, who, once she had me in her clutches, began to play with me like a cat plays with a mouse. She tested our friendship and disrespected me in ways I had never experienced. She excluded my 9-year-old son from her son's birthday party, justifying her actions by telling me that my child was less popular and therefore not worthy of friendship with her more social child. She mocked the *New York Times* best-seller that I chose for book club and accused me of projecting my Catholic faith on to others. I smiled and said with a laugh, "It didn't pick it because it was Catholic, it received five-star reviews."

Carol also thought it was funny to teach her children Italian profanity, which they used freely, instructing other children on the Italian word for "shit." There was something sinister about Carol's energy and being around it felt like a poisonous snake was lurking nearby. As I denied the toxicity of her venomous bites and continued to tolerate her devious manipulation, I had to admit that her passive aggressive behavior extended outward into the community, as she had a pattern of slandering anyone who challenged her beliefs or her children's behavior. Earlier in our friendship, she had boasted that she intentionally ran over the orange traffic cones in our school's carpool pick-up line to get back at the principal for punishing her son. He had been the ringleader of a food flight at the Dolphin Diner, our school's Cafeteria. She also complained that our school's teachers were biased against her children. Carol's energy zapped me and did not make me feel good. I had disconnected from my essential self and needed to Claim new alliances that mirrored who I wanted to be as a mother and as a friend.

As I began to back away from our friendship, Carol made efforts to win me back. I was kind, but politely declined her invitations. It was time for me to recalibrate and align with the energy inside my heart. Like any break-up, it was challenging because our lives overlapped. We belonged to the same swim and tennis club and socialized at the same events. But I knew that the cost of the alliance was too expensive because it triggered below the line feelings of inadequacy not only in me, but in my children. Her energy clashed with mine and I could no longer be Carol's victim, pawn, or fool. Claiming me meant upgrading my energy by being pickier about who I invited into my sacred circle of trust. When you try to be loved by everyone, it makes it harder for you to love yourself. We must always insist on friendships where there is mutual respect, trust, honesty, and a willingness to connect as equals in the relationship.

Everything in life is about the energy frequency you decide to Claim. The way you feel around certain people will tell you if the connection is a good one or if it needs to be released. The energy around our relationships is about a chemical connectivity. Like electrons, we are either attracted to someone's energy field or repelled by it. Listen when your intuition tells you to "stand clear"—energy vibrations do not lie. Yes, we must always be kind, but as my mother has always said, "Be nice, but you don't have to get all arms about the neck with them."

We all need to be comfortable releasing people from our lives. Not just the ones that break our hearts, but the benign relationships that have gone out of style. A chance encounter you have with someone from your past can feel like eating a glazed donut, although the first bite tickles your tongue, after the encounter, an emptiness sits in your stomach like a lump of wet dough, sugary and gluttonous. We feel under nourished, the energy of the bond now extinct. It doesn't diminish any of the memories, but they are behind you, an archive of the past. Why do we struggle to release these expired connections? Although in their time they were the spectacular fireworks of our reality, they have faded, a cherished relic of who we once were.

The more internal work you do to align with your essential self, the easier it becomes to release stale energy so you can Claim the new upgraded energy that mirrors who you are becoming. Not everyone comes into your life to stay forever. For those who only stay a short while, we must be grateful for what they bestow upon us.

Have you ever had an instant energy connection with someone? It's magical and feels like an alliance that was destined to be. Pam's instant energy connection happened in the story of meeting her husband, Mike, who crashed her elegant Christmas party, an extra stag-along with nothing better to do on a Saturday night. Although it sounds like a Hallmark romance, each time she tells me the story, I am both entranced and enchanted that there is still such a thing as an instant connection. "When he walked into the room our eyes met, and I remembered we had attended the same college, but I never knew him well. As we approached one another, I introduced myself again and suddenly everyone else in the room became insignificant, it was only Mike and me. I locked into his gaze and that was it, a connection of the heart." I know what you are thinking, too good to be true, but you're wrong. Her husband, Mike, tells the exact same story. Proof that true connection is a magical alchemy of energy attraction, meant to be and for a purpose, and not just about romantic love.

If we are lucky, we have people in our lives that intertwine with our energy so naturally that we can be separated from them for years and then pick up right where we left off. These connections are rare and require that we receive that person's energy in a transformed state of evolution. You are not the same person that you were in high school, in your late twenties, during your childbearing years, or after you decide to live a sober life. The more clarity we have on what serves our energy, the easier it is to create a protective energy bubble around the parts of ourselves that we hope to preserve for ourselves and those we love.

As I have softened with age, I have developed a discerning eye for those who deserve to be placed on my A-List of alliances. An A-list is a finite gathering of advisors that you have Claimed and trust emphatically. In Brené Brown's book, *Dare to Lead*, she calls this small cluster her "Square Squad" or the few people in life whose opinion really matters to her. For me, A-Listers are the people who are on my same frequency and who leave me feeling energized after I have spent time with them. They inspire me, help me learn new things and remind me to be brave. Most importantly, my A-Listers hold my secrets and vulnerabilities with both love and compassion, as I do with theirs. My A-Listers know who they are.

The most evolutionary relationships that exist in our lives are those we have with our children and our aging parents. While at times it seems challenging, as these relationships span our entire life, from birth to death. We love them but sometimes don't like them, and it can take an entire lifetime to Claim the ideal relationship we want to have with them. The reason that we find the Claim step so difficult is that not only do we share DNA, but we often have them to thank for our wounds and false identities. They have the ability to bring out the worst in us and the power to conjure emotions we never knew existed. For me, they are my cherished clan and although sometimes they drive me nutty, we have banded together so we can survive in the world. It is a familial bond that restricts my ability to be genuinely objective towards anyone who threatens a member of my family, especially in times of struggle. When it comes to my people, I am loyal, tribal, and a bit codependent, for they have taught me everything I know about love and managing relationships.

My adult son, Patrick, and I approach the world differently and have always operated on divergent energy frequencies. While he was growing up, we had our fair share of scrimmages about "how" and "at what pace" things should be completed. This started in his livewire toddler days and extended all the way through to his senior year in high school. It felt like trying to keep a spirited colt contained in a corral, he was going buck and kick until we opened the gate and set him free. Over a decade ago, as he packed for college, an overt reminder spilled from my mouth and he snapped back defiantly, "MOM, BACK OFF!"

It was a pivotal moment in our relationship and one I will never forget. I had lovingly nurtured him for 18 years and all he was asking of me was to trust that everything he needed was already inside him. His request for autonomy made our adjustment to his college years, and his life ever after, much more manageable. He has taught me that more is "caught than taught" and that most of your child's crucial learning happens when they fail. Our children actually pick up a lot of world knowledge by watching how their parents manage adversity. We must Claim that we have led them well and then separate ourselves, our expectations, and our energy from our adult children. Everyone must learn "adulting" the old-fashioned way, and this energy boundary does not mean that we, as parents, stop worrying, hoping, and praying for our grown children, it only means that we offer them the same self-sovereignty that we offer ourselves. If you are lucky, these emerging adults may ask for your opinion. Think about what you wish someone had told you when you were younger and then offer them the abridged version. I guarantee, if they need more counsel from you, they will ask for the details.

Aging parents are a whole different paradigm shift that nature does not adequately prepare us for. Suddenly the people who offered you unsolicited counsel are calling for advice on everything from downloading books on Audible to how to deal with slanderous email communications. My mother, Rosemary, is 88-years old, and I talk to her almost every day. One morning she called me, having received a nasty text from an ex-in-law. When she shared the content and the context of the message, I found myself reaching for both my sword and my shield. Our roles have reversed: I am now *her* protector. Knowing that it would do no good for me to slay the sender of the text, my first instinct was to protect my mother from her worry and help her to Claim a way to detach from the toxicity of the issue. My intent was to ground myself in my own energy and then attempt to neutralize my mother's emotions.

As we continued our discussion, I began to ask questions and get curious, so I could better advise her. Before I went into full coach mode, I caught myself, knowing that a daughter cannot be objective. I cast-off my professional identity and instead, Claimed familial love and fierce loyalty. All anyone is looking for is love, safety, and belonging. My mother needed love, so I listened and received her anxiety. My mother required safety, so I made suggestions on how she might create boundaries for herself. My mother also needed to belong, so I accepted that, for my mother, this meant being loyal to her family, even her ex-family members. She talked about her values around kindness and how important it was for her to be compassionate to everyone, even those who threw stones her way. What I heard was that her desire to be kind was stronger than her desire to create an energetic boundary. I asked her what she most feared: "Being unkind," she said. "I can't be unpleasant to people, even mean people. It's not my nature."

My mother is a giver. Our discussion had illuminated that her generosity had been compromised by the negative energy, now rattling her cage. Ignoring nastiness and leaning into the greater good of situations has always been one of her superpowers. It is what makes her an incredible mother, grandmother, and friend. She calls it her missionary work, always giving everyone the benefit of the doubt and choosing to do the right thing. This superpower, however, had now placed her between a rock and a hard place and dangerously close to a below the line response. She had been drawn into someone else's argument, had no place to hide and no easy solution. We talked about what she could do to honor her values while also detaching herself from an issue that was not hers to solve. It wasn't my problem to solve either (Remember, not my circus not my monkeys!).

Here is where I must be honest with you, I had to resist the temptation to resort into my past tendencies to react with below the line masculine behavior (like trying to control someone else's outcome). My mother and I considered all the options, and together, came up with a solution that she found acceptable. In it, I heard her stand gracefully resolute in kindness. She joyfully changed the subject, clearly ready to get on with her day.

My internal conflict remained, however, and I felt myself restraining my masculine warring-warrior energy and a desire to build a metaphorical wall around my mother's kind heart so I could protect her from herself, but that was not what she needed from me that day. She was only asking me to see, hear, and accept her for who she is, a kind and loving person who is doing the best she can. Over time, with this work, you will get better at resisting urges to save, control, and fix things for the people you love. Part of loving someone is listening to their truth and respecting their wishes. So, what I guess am sharing, is that self-sovereignty serves our relationships with our children and aging parents too. Ground in yourself first and then work your way out from there.

It's not your job to be liked by every person on this planet. Your job is simply to be yourself and Claim your truth. Claiming is the act of practicing self-sovereignty by choosing to take responsibility for your own stuff, like noticing the triggers and fears of your inner critic and having an acute awareness not only of the limits of your energy reserves, but when someone has infiltrated your energetic boundaries. When we remember that the negative energy of others is their stuff and has nothing to do with us, it makes it easy to detach from it. I know that this is often easier said than done, that's why we must always try to receive ourselves with self-compassion, acceptance, and a sense of humor. Life is messy, relationships are complex, and sometimes outcomes are uncertain. When you have clarity and Claim your truth, the right people and things will find you.

CHAPTER FIVE

Preparing for The Reframe

DEFINING YOUR CORE VALUES

IN ORDER TO PREPARE FOR OUR REFRAME, WHICH IS THE final step in the reshaping of our new paradigm of thinking, we need to re-align again with our core values. Whether or not you have previously identified the why behind your core beliefs, your values will most definitely shift through the awareness of your triggers, false identities, and core wounds. I am speaking of YOUR core values, not the moral or ethical standards of society. We are unearthing what makes you unique as a human. Your core values are the fundamental beliefs that shape your personal boundaries, your ability to say a kind, but resolute "HELL NO" and the container with which you choose to live your life.

The root and source of our core values starts from birth, the age-old question of nature versus nurture. You were likely born with certain innate core values, the shaping of which occurred through the influence of your parents and other significant mentors, friends, media/current events, and life experiences. While some values continue to align with the foundation of who we are becoming, others need to be modified or eliminated completely because they were created within false identities and no longer fit who you are. Anyone who commits to a new mindset, like sobriety, healthy living, or parenthood, understands well that there will be growing pains and voids that need to be filled along the way. Just as a child outgrows their shoe size, as we evolve, we upgrade and redesign our values system.

There is no question that our parents have the most influence on the initial imprinting of our foundational core values. Much of who you become happens during the developmental stages of birth to age five. In most cases, your parents greatly influenced what you heard and saw. Loyalty to the family clan became one of my core values because I watched my father serve as the trusted advisor to not only my grandparents, but to a plethora of great aunts and great uncles. I have a tribal heart and though I have Named and Claimed boundaries around how I engage with my family of origin, my loyalty towards them means that I will always show up when my family is in need.

We also experience significant relationships with adults other than our parents, such as grandparents, family friends, teachers, coaches, and religious leaders. My parents invited an eclectic group of adults into our lives when we were children. One of my favorites was my father's accountant, Dan, who without children of his own, became a beloved and adopted mentor to my brothers and me. I also had two special friends of my mother's that I called my "Fairy Godmothers". Throughout my life they told me that things would be all right but far more importantly, they consistently told me that I was all right. Connections with a surrogate-bonus parent can have a significant impact on a young person, influencing their lives with opportunities, perspectives, and much needed guidance.

When you begin school, your peer group becomes a huge part of the core values you take on. After developing a close-knit friend group during my elementary school years, I felt unhinged after my parents moved us to a new town with better schools. I became a floater and tried on lots of varied peer groups all through middle school. Although I felt like an outsider, I learned about the structure of social groups, the kind of friends I could trust and who I needed to release. It wasn't until I started high school that I could Claim the value of belonging. Cross country, track, and cheerleading opened doors for me, not only socially, but by teaching me that connection and community will find you when you do what you love.

Along with the people in your life, events, both positive and negative, shape your core values. A person who overcame obstacles and earned a scholarship to an Ivy League college, someone who loses a parent at a young age or a gifted young athlete who achieves notoriety at the Olympics, will all be shaped by different values based on their unique life story. Although, we can share values despite different life paths, our experiences, the opportunities we have available to us, and the choices we make, all impact who we become. Because I was a struggling reader, I have incredible discipline and work hard at everything that I undertake. Once a core wounding, I now see the importance of hard work and education, and it drives my mindset towards the how, what, and why of anything that I pursue.

Values guide our behaviors, the decisions we make, the alliances we choose and the actions that we undertake. Values ground us in our life purpose and help us gain clarity about what's most important to us. Sometimes values show up strongest when we experience dissonance, like being overlooked, snubbed, or disrespected. The experience I shared in Chapter Four about my doomed friendship with Carol was jarring to me because she tromped on my values around respect and protecting those that we hold dear. Another example could be an altercation with an elderly parent who questions your child rearing style, forcing you to question how your parent failed you and how you are failing your children. The values we hear most often from families are respect, love, responsibility, and consistency, and kids learn through our example. We cannot just tell our kids to be respectful, we must model respect by honoring our elders with humility and patience.

Some battles are not worth fighting. When my values clash with someone I love, I take time to think about the costs of going into battle. With my parents and my adult children, it is usually about my desire to control their life choices, and truthfully, those decisions are none of my business. On the other hand, if your coworker poaches on your project, going to the mat in a Gentle Warrior Way, helps you to honor your integrity.

When I begin to work with a coaching client, I ask what their values are. They might list high level themes like authenticity, compassion, trust, integrity, etc. However, as we work together, these core values get more defined. Understanding that your core values are much more nuanced than just listing ideals. They are the sum of "the secret why" behind our core beliefs.

So how does one go about discovering their core values?

When a client shows up in session agitated or troubled, I might ask them, "What core value was stepped on or disrespected?" The query helps us get to root of the issue, so we can Name the emotion they are feeling and help them to get to the other side of it. While it is not our preferred portal, dissonant experiences are one of the best ways to raise your conscientiousness about which core values are most important and why something you encountered has pushed you so sorely out of your comfort zone.

Tatum, a client who lives in New York City, arrived our very first Zoom together, both infuriated and deeply saddened. Earlier that morning Tatum had gone to CVS specifically to buy Covid tests because she was worried about the health for her family. As she waited outside for the store to open, she stood alongside two other individuals that she assumed had the same intent. What she discovered however, was quite the opposite. As the store opened for business, the two people waiting beside Tatum rushed in ahead and began indiscriminately sweeping the shelves into their coat and suitcase. "I was in total shock that the clerks just looked away, doing nothing. Now as I am feeling so out of control about the virus, this violation of such basic core values really gets to me. Not to mention that this kind of disrespectful looting will be dismissed with no ramifications or jail time. To be honest with you, I find the state of our city both discouraging and disgusting," she declared with true anguish in her eyes.

What followed in our session was a deep discussion about how the extreme disparity of the incident had not only invaded the borders of Tatum's personal core values but also how the act of witnessing the incident had blatantly disrespected the societal norms she thought were sacred. Like getting punched in the stomach unexpectedly, we are left breathless, unsure of how to comprehend what just happened. Taking time to process the event and identify the core values that were violated, helped Tatum to Name the emotion so she could understand the why behind it. The story I shared about my mother receiving the slanderous text cut into the core of my values around family loyalty. I felt a raw outrage that initially triggered a reactive, below the line response to protect someone I loved. Anytime you, someone you love or something you care about is threatened, it hurts because it hits a value nerve. If we begin to understand the why of the trigger, it helps us to Name the value and process the "what" and the "why" that has rubbed up against our core belief system.

Look at the chart below and circle the core values that are most important to you. What are your "must haves"? Don't overthink it, simply choose the five values that you must honor to be aligned with the integrity of your essential self. Please note that my list is by no means complete, if you think of a value that is not on the list, please add it. When it comes to core values there is no right or wrong-only who we are. As you begin to Name emotion and Claim the values you want to keep sacred in your life, your Gentle Warrior core values list will expand and grow.

CORE VALUES

- Accomplishment
- Acknowledgment
- Adventure
- Altruism
- Authenticity
- Awe
- Balance
- Beauty
- Boldness
- Calm
- Challenge
- Collaboration
- Commitment
- Community
- Compassion
- Comradeship
- Confidence
- Connectedness
- Consistency
- Contentment
- Contribution
- Cooperation
- Courage
- Creativity
- Curiosity
- Determination
- Dependability
- Directness
- Discovery
- Ease
- Education
- Efficiency
- Empowerment

- Enthusiasm
- Environment
- Equality
- Ethics
- Excellence
- Fairness
- Faith
- Flexibility
- Focus
- Forgiveness
- Freedom
- Friendship
- Fun
- Generosity
- Grace
- Gratitude
- Growth
- Happiness
- Harmony
- Health
- Helpfulness
- Honesty
- Honor
- Humility
- Humor
- Idealism
- Imagination
- Independence
- Individuality
- Innovation
- Integrity
- Intelligence
- Insight

- Intuition
- Joy
- Kindness
- Leadership
- Learning
- Listening
- Love
- Loyalty
- Modesty
- Open-Mindedness
- Optimism
- Organization
- Partnership
- Passion
- Patience
- Peace
- Professionalism
- Radiance
- Reliability
- Respect
- Responsibility
- Spirituality
- Self-Reliance
- Thoughtfulness
- Trustworthy
- Understanding
- Unity
- Vitality
- Versatility
- Vision
- Vulnerability
- Warmth
- Wisdom

Exploring Your Edges

Values are the personal, intimate, and internal barometers of what's important to a person and what isn't. In my workshops I use the mini values reflection that follows to help clients explore the edges of their value boundaries. While these queries most always yield the best insights when they are shared back and forth in conversation with another human, I hope that the introspection can point you toward the values that are most sacred to you. If you have opportunity, I encourage you to invite a thought partner into your discussion. There is treasure to be harvested as every experience, good or bad, can become a priceless learning opportunity.

MINI VALUES REFLECTION

Part 1: Name the last time you got extremely upset with a person or a situation. Perhaps you had an argument, an altercation or like Tatum witnessed something disturbing. What was it about? What was going on for you? The specific details of the incident are not important here, instead reflect about what was triggered:

- I felt powerless.
- I felt judged.
- I felt unseen or unheard.
- I felt unsafe.
- I felt excluded.
- I felt blamed.

- I felt disrespected.
- I felt unloved.
- I felt controlled or manipulated.
- I felt trapped.
- I felt like I couldn't speak my truth.

When we encounter anything that pushes our buttons or makes us frustrated, we gain awareness about our "deal breakers". Anything that brings disgrace upon the integrity of who you are helps you to gain clarity on not only which values were being stepped on and not honored, but how you might be strategic in Naming and Claiming a more Gentle Warrior response in the future.

Now let's flip it:

Part 2: Name the last time that you felt deeply fulfilled, grateful or completely at one with yourself and your life. This "Peak Experience"* could be a specific event, a time where you experienced a total state of presence, when traveling or performing a routine task that conjured gratitude. The key ingredient to this moment is that it was

* Maslow, 1954

significant and felt meaningful and fulfilling. You felt love, ease, even bliss. You were not being judged, and you were not judging yourself. You accepted everything as it was, feeling a sense of wholeness and connection to what really matters to you. Most importantly, you felt fully at peace with yourself. This is closest we can get to "being" with our essential selves.

What was going on for you?

- I felt honored and respected.
- I felt connected to someone or something.
- I felt a sense of inner peace.
- I felt appreciation and/or gratitude.
- I felt pride and/or accomplishment.
- I felt confident and in flow with my natural gifts.
- I felt that I was grounded and aligned with what is most important.

Notice that Part 2 of this inquiry, where you were honoring your core values, strikes an emotional chord inside you. Peak experiences are often described as transcendent moments of pure grace and elation. These moments stand out from everyday events because they leave a lasting impression. They are spiritual in nature, and we have reverence for them because they help us get in touch with what is most important: the foundation of our core beliefs, our values. Abraham Maslow's hierarchy of needs is a theory of motivation which states that five categories of human needs dictate an individual's behavior. Those needs are physiological needs, safety needs, love and belonging needs, esteem needs, and self-actualization needs.

MASLOW'S HIERARCHY OF NEEDS

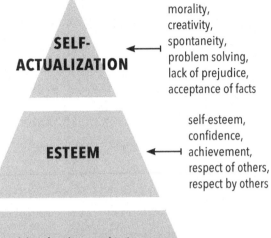

SELF-ACTUALIZATION ← morality, creativity, spontaneity, problem solving, lack of prejudice, acceptance of facts

ESTEEM ← self-esteem, confidence, achievement, respect of others, respect by others

friendship, family, sexual intimacy
LOVE/BELONGING

security of body, of employment, of resources, of morality, of the family, of health, of property
SAFETY

breathing, food, water, sex, sleep, homeostasis, excretion
PHYSIOLOGICAL

"Human life will never be understood unless its highest aspirations are taken into account. Growth, self-actualization, the striving toward health, the quest for identity and autonomy, the yearning for excellence (and other ways of phrasing the striving "upward") must by now be accepted beyond question as a widespread and perhaps universal human tendency . . . "

— ABRAHAM MASLOW,
Motivation and Personality

In his work, Maslow considered our peak experience to be an indication of self-actualization. A moment where we feel connected to our purest form of identity, our essential self. The aftereffects of the peak experience leave the individual seeing themselves and the world in a new way. They are able to view themselves positively and see their lives as worthwhile and meaningful. The peak experience is an exhibition of Maslow's emphasis on the quest for growth maximizing potential as the true goal of human existence.

Core Values will always bubble up when something resonates deep within us or when the integrity of a value boundary is threatened. We cannot run from our truth and values are the innate primal reminders of the virtues that live deep within our heart. Naming the emotions that are woven within these core beliefs help us to protect their borders and give us the tools to stand resolutely in above the line Gentle Warrior resourcefulness.

When a person understands more fully their unique values and how the those core beliefs came to resonate within them, they can use a past experience as a touchstone to further fortify their belief system. Brian's values emerged brilliantly when he shared his experience of a college trip he had taken to South Africa. Travel conjured what

Brian described as a his "Carpe Diem" mindset and he noted that with this particular group of close friends he was not only a confident risk taker, but he saw himself as "enough". He felt seen, heard, and loved unconditionally. The themes of gratitude, connection, courage, and authenticity illuminated more values that Brian wanted to call forth in his life: empowerment, trust, collaboration with a like-minded community, and respect for himself. We revisited his "South African" perspective many times, extracting essential parts of him that he had forgotten existed. Brian found a favorite photograph from this trip and framed it as a visual reminder of the core values he hoped to call in and embody going forward. "I love this photo because I am in the center, surrounded by all of my friends, and feeling at peace with myself. It reminds me that when I connect to my courage and authenticity, I project that good energy out into the world and comes back to me even stronger. I am enough!"

As you probably have experienced in your own life, it is the everyday rituals and routines that help to ground us in our values. Each morning I rise pre-dawn and take a walk with my husband and our dog, Mags. It has become a spiritual practice that solidifies our bond with each other as we enjoy a peaceful moment of presence together before we start our workday. This simple COVID-inspired ritual grounds me in my values every day, plus I get to witness the sunrise with someone I love. There is gratitude for our connection, grace in the optimism of a new day dawning, and an open mindedness that conjures a more expanded perspective for the simple things that bring richness into our lives. If there is an emotion that either one of us needs to Name, we create a safe space of trust so we might help each other Claim a softer, more intentional way through it. Rituals like this one help to root us in what is most important, making the journey of life more fulfilling, meaningful, and joyous. Plus, being clear on how we are lined up with our core values reduces stress, frustration, resentment, guilt, shame, and anger. Sounds like a good thing to get clear on, doesn't it?

A teacher to the core, I created the visual (below) to illustrate in my workshops how our core values are the gatekeepers to both our energetic boundaries and ultimately our internal energy reserves. A simplified representation, consistent with "Maslow's Hierarchy of Needs", this diagram demonstrates how core value violations and energetic boundary breaches can impact and threaten the sanctuary of our internal energy reserves (Remember: Chapter Four's discussion on creating energetic boundaries, on page 71), leaving us feeling emotionally depleted and vulnerable to below the line reactivity. Even before we can Name the emotion we are feeling, our bodies often react with a physical response: a tightening in the shoulders, a knot in the stomach or a consuming fatigue that we can't explain.

The truth is that most people aren't fully aware of their values, and they don't honor them as much as they could, even after they have identified them. Through the years, they have developed strong coping strategies, often bearing huge disharmony in life because they believe, "that's just the way it is." Yet, when we aren't intentional about noticing when someone or something tromps our values, it's hard to live a life in alignment with them. This is why, once we are clear on the "why" behind our core values, it is much easier to have the courage to create boundaries so we can stay aligned with our integrity . Sadly, society encourages us to "swallow our pride," "bite the bullet," or "endure" rather than honoring our values by stepping out of our comfort zone, standing in uncomfortableness and speaking up about what we are feeling.

The Choice is Yours: Is it a HELL NO or a HOLY YES?

Saying "No" to what is not part of your value system is the next bold step towards your Reframe. Learning the power of "no" is as important as learning that saying "yes" can actually be the most effective way to honor yourself. I know that this sounds confusing, so let me explain. For many of us, just the act of saying no is one of life's most difficult challenges. When I am helping clients to stand more confidently in their values, I often challenge them to say "no" five times in one week and then send me a stop sign emoji each time they triumphantly stand in a resolute "no." Although daring them to say "no" is an incredible learning opportunity, some of them refuse this challenge, afraid of the consequences, "I don't think I can do that, what if someone pushes back?" Others, intrigued by the possibility of taking their power back agree, "I'll try it three times but I don't know." "Yes, I need to be more forceful. I can't wait to see the look on their faces!"

There is so much wrapped up in saying "no." You are disappointing someone, and your people pleasing inner critic wakes up screaming, "Warning, we are leaving the safety zone!"

When we say a reluctant "yes" instead of "no", we are avoiding the possibility of a 15-second uncomfortable moment with whoever is asking us for the thing we really don't want to do. Obviously, if your boss asks you to do a task you dread, you might have to do it, but if a neighbor asks you to babysit their unruly flock of fledglings for the weekend, you do have the power to say a kind but clear, "no thank you." It comes down to your ability to tolerate those 15-seconds of feeling uncomfortable. Taking the "yes" option is a bigger commitment; you experience resentment for agreeing to do the thing you do not want to do. As Bréne Brown says: "Choose discomfort over resentment."

After waving my speaking fee for a local fund-raising event, one of the women in the audience reached out to ask if I would be the featured speaker for her university alumni group, (made up, by the way, of retired senior citizens). Before I had a chance to call her back, she emailed me with a second request, assuming that I would also be waving my speaker fee as an alumnus of the university. Every bone in my body screamed a resounding "HELL NO!" A group of 75 to 90-year-old women, although lovely, are not my target audience and my time and value as a paid speaker is much too precious. I wrote her back a kind reply, thanking her for the honor, and explaining that waving my speaking fee for the fund raising event was a one-off donation to support a philanthropic cause. When she emailed me again, giving me all reasons why speaking to her group for free was an incredible opportunity for me to give back to the university and highlight my coaching practice, I stood bravely in the uncomfortable feeling of disappointing someone. "Thank for thinking of me, but my final answer is no." Do I regret my decision? Absolutely not. I would have spent valuable energy, leading up to this 45-minute talk, steeped in resentment and anger at myself for not honoring the integrity of my truth.

"No" is a power word. It gives us a definite sense of self. This means that saying "no" is an ideal opportunity to rediscover your values, priorities, and sense of who you are. Until we learn to say "no" we will continue to be overwhelmed with too much to do and not enough time. Have you noticed how NOT saying "no" impacts quality time with yourself, family and your health and stress levels? Throughout my life, there have been times where I have agreed to take part in activities that did not match me or my values. I struggled with a fear of my worthiness that was fueled by a people pleasing inner critic that I have lovingly named, Sister Mary Francis. I picture Sister Mary Francis, as a kind and harmless little nun. Although, she always has good intentions, she is the voice in my head that does not like to disappoint anyone. She does not guard my boundaries and is convinced that I am not kind, friendly or thoughtful enough. No offense to my dear mother, but Sister Mary Francis may embody some of my mother's reminders from when I was young, "Be nice, Andrea."

In my younger days, Sister Mary Francis yielded great power. I would hear myself saying "yes" instead of a resounding, "HELL, NO!" The Mary Francis factor impacted my judgement about certain friendships, volunteer jobs that I had no time to do, and tasks at work that did not serve me or my vision for the future. I have got Mary Francis figured out now though, so when she shows up reminding me that it would be awfully nice for me to "bite the bullet" and speak to my university's alumni group, I counter: "Oh, hi Sister! I know you are suggesting that I am committing elder

abuse by disappointing these sweet older women, but I know what is best for me and my energy levels. By standing in a kind but firm 'no, thank you,' I am creating a boundary and honoring my values of confidence, self-empowerment, independence, directness, idealism, integrity, and peace of mind."

Just like that, I embraced and honored six core values and created a kind, but clear boundary for myself and my level of stress. I would venture to guess that you might have your own form of Sister Mary Francis lurking around in your subconsciousness. Call her out and tell her respectfully that you have decided to sit this next "should" out. Whether you learn to say "no" more often, or just learn to say "yes" on your terms, it's time to release yourself from the burden of pleasing others. Give yourself the time and freedom to do what matters most to you. As we process and practice the power of "no", we begin to understand how Naming and Claiming dances so very elegantly with the values we are honoring. Imagine the power you could get back for yourself by just by saying "Hell No."

Take the one-week challenge by practicing saying "no" when you really mean "HELL NO" and watch how people respond. There are people out there who will not take "no" for an answer. Trust yourself to stand firm in the 15 seconds of uncomfortableness and see what you learn. Chances are the more you practice saying a kind but clear "no", the easier it will become and the more you will begin to train people to respect your boundaries.

There is another side of "no" where you find yourself saying "no" when a simple "yes" would serve you better. We all know the people that refuse to accept kind offers to do them a simple favor. It almost feels like they don't trust you or that your offer is not sincere. There is grace in receiving kindness, and sometimes saying a "Holy Yes" actually helps you to honor the person gifting you their kindness.

I once had someone offer me a $400.00 credit on a monthly bill because they had repeatedly overcharged my credit card three months running. After the third time of respectfully calling them out on the oversight, they were so embarrassed at the disconnect between the service they were providing and their inept billing process, that they offered me a month's credit. The offer shocked me, and I heard myself say, "No, I can't accept that." What was I thinking, and why couldn't I say yes? Truthfully, it was my feelings of unworthiness again. Even though I had been outraged by the repeated overcharging, in each instance they had immediately credited me back the overage. By accepting their kind offer, I worried that their motivation might wane, or the level of service might be compromised if I didn't pay full market price. With reluctance, I did accept their kind offer and you know what happened? My respect for the integrity with which they conducted business grew leaps and bounds. They stood behind their sincere apology, their policies, and the excellence of the service I was buying. I felt seen, heard, and respected. "Holy YES and thank you so much for your kindness," I said, and I meant it.

If someone offers to do something for you to make up for a mistake or just to be nice, say a "HOLY Yes," and stand in the power of "thank you." Own the yes, and honor people with trust that they are making a choice within their value boundaries.

Try on each of these scenarios in the context of the power of "NO" and find your own yes traps:

- When you're stressed or overwhelmed

- When you're already doing too much

- When you're tired or sick

- When it's someone else's issue

- When you feel taken for granted

- When it's something you do not want to do

Learning to say "HELL NO" to the things that do not honor our values means that you have more room to say a "HOLY YES" to the things that do!

Making the decision to create a boundary is less about wielding power over others and more about a protective practice that contributes to your emotional and physical health. While learning to say a polite "no, thank you" is a start, as we emotionally mature through the Name and Claim steps, we get to play within the variances and discrepancies within our values system. We will be able to appreciate and tolerate more unique circumstances within the newly defined boundaries of our integrity, our sanity, and our privacy. Life is not always black and white, and clarity of our core beliefs is imperative to navigate variances and maintain our own ethical conduct (I won't do x because it does not match my value around y), or to measure when someone has trumped a value that we hold dear (being seen, heard, respected, having autonomy, etc.). Although it feels rotten when someone tramples over one of our value boundaries, we can use the insight from a dissonant experience of the past to right a wrong or take it less personally.

Defining a client archetype was the boundary that I put in place to guard the integrity of my coaching practice and to protect the value I place on my business. My experience is that 25% of potential clients get cold feet, even after saying "yes" to coaching in our initial sample session. Their primal need to survive keeps them from stepping out of their comfort zone. After an expansive conversation where they commit to investing in themselves and their vision for the future, when I send some potential clients a coaching agreement, they go either "radio silent" or email back that they are not ready. I try not to take these changes of heart personally, understanding that it is all part of the "fear factor." Although a guide can light the way, a person must be willing to take a risk if they are to walk their true path. My ideal clients all have one common denominator: they are brave and they are ready. They want to create change in their life and make things happen. Real change takes courage, and courage means taking risks.

When I was a new coach, I had not yet learned that the magic ingredient for a successful coaching relationship is synergy—a mutually advantageous conjunction between two people towards a common goal. In other words, coach and client have to connect as people first, they have to like my energy and I have to like theirs. What I had to learn fairly quickly in order to be of the best service, was to set clear boundaries with the energy of a client. If I don't feel a connection with someone during our initial conversation, there is a loss of integrity on my end because I lose my ability to "move" a person towards their life goals. Believe it or not, I can decern my ability to be an effective guide (or not) within the first five minutes of a sample session conversation. When we are grounded in what we *can* control (our own behavior) and what we *cannot* control (the emotional angst of another), we separate ourselves from the situation by creating a boundary. Like the energetic boundary practices discussed in Chapter Four, we must first ground in our own energy and the values we hope to honor if we are to live within the integrity of our core beliefs. The more clarity we have around the "why" behind our core beliefs, the easier it is to catch ourselves before we dip below the line.

I also intentionally use somatic tools, moving people into different perspectives, asking them what anxiety or fear feels like in their body, or prompting them to dream of what their future might look like if they could not fail. Some people resist these activities, or they do not like to transfer their thoughts into actions and these kind of thinkers are not a good fit for me. I am confident that I am a powerful coach, but also certain that I am not the best coach for everyone. Once I created the boundary of attracting the right clients for the sake of both my time and their time, sample sessions became a screening process for me, not the potential client. If I don't feel an instant connection with someone, I offer them a referral to one of my colleagues. Helping people find the right coach is more important to me than winning the sale. Referring clients also honors my values around the generosity of supporting colleagues in our coaching community.

One of the best ways to get clear on our boundaries and solidify our core values is to explore the intricacies of their borders. Integrity is the bridge between being and doing. Dissonant experiences with resistant clients informed the borders of my values around who I have decided to coach. However, exchanges with our family are far more complicated in their entangled histories and have a way of conjuring a reactive darkness that can skew our alignment with our essential self. While we tell ourselves that we are grounded and calm, one unexpected quarrel can threaten not only our boundaries, but the values within them. Your teenager might call you a "bitch" in the heat of the moment. The sting is bad, and the false identity is hard to stand in because it doesn't match who you think you are. Being reactive by matching the anger of an emotional teen does not align with who you want to be, so now what? After you feel the unsavory identity settle under your skin, integrity helps with what to Name and Claim:

- "What am I feeling?"
- "What do I say or do next?"

You try to understand your child's adolescent anguish. Name what your child can't tolerate or "be with." What value can you Claim and offer up to bridge the chasm? Chances are that the name calling does not align with your teenager's integrity either. When trying to negotiate with anger, it is always best to wait until both parties have calmed down. When we allow space to reflect (NAME: feel and think), the action that we take (CLAIM: saying and/or doing) will match up more authentically with our values and boundaries. Even if your action is not received in the positive light that you anticipated, choosing to Claim a value (love, connection, compassion, safety) helps you stand resolutely in the integrity of the action.

I abruptly left a toddler's birthday celebration after one of my offspring (I won't say whom) defiantly tested my earlier threat that if they continued their unacceptable behavior, we would have to leave the party. As rude as it seemed at the time, I had to follow through with it. When I called the hostess later to apologize for our rapid exit, she applauded me for standing firm. After the incident, my children took me at my word. What story are you telling yourself and how might you detach from the feeling that has hooked or triggered the shadow-version of yourself?

Maggie, who worked as a highly paid consultant, shared her feelings of failing a client whose anxiety was so great it inhibited their (and Maggie's) ability to act on the project that she had been hired to remedy. Maggie blamed herself for the client's inaction and found that her value boundaries clashed with her professional integrity as Maggie felt responsible for the client's trepidation and anguish. By naming ("What am I feeling?") the unsavory identity of being perceived as an overpriced and ineffective consultant, Maggie was able to release the false identity and Claim an action that better matched her core values. "What do I say or do next to help this client achieve their goal?" These prompts helped Maggie ground in her own energy and core values so that she could separate herself from her client's panic. When Maggie reminded herself that she was not part of the client's problem, but rather a first responder to help rescue the client, Maggie was able to show up to meetings honoring her values around being a calm, collected and professional consultant, which was exactly what her client needed to reach a resolution. This new perspective also helped Maggie to ground herself in the poised wisdom, and experienced counsel that she brought to her clients,.

Your new life is going to cost you your old one. You have Named your core wounds and Claimed new identities. You have quieted your inner critic, and you are test driving newfound core values. You also have a better sense of how to defend your energetic boundaries. You are a new you, and some people will embrace how you show up differently and others will not like the change (because it forces them to look at what they need to change). You have entered the weeding out process, or as I call it, the Reframe. I have prepped you for this last step, to walk out into the world as a Gentle Warrior and stand up to new tests and unexplored environments. While it seems daunting, I assure you, great freedom lies ahead on your path.

CHAPTER SIX

Reframe

ARE YOU READY TO TAKE UP MORE SPACE AND BOLDLY stand in your core values? Because if so, you will be subject to new tests. You have changed. You are no longer the same. The Universe will be more than happy to provide you with people who will help you practice your new mindset. They will gladly offer feedback or criticism, and challenging opportunities with which you can practice new, above the line responses, boundary checks, and make peace with your triggers. You are in the final step to becoming a Gentle Warrior: The Reframe.

Although I have always been conscientious and intentional in my actions, up until four years ago, I had never practiced mindfulness, let alone attempted a Reframe. I was all about masculine efficiency and, not surprisingly, my steadfast goal to find speedy solutions to the conflicts that I encountered sometimes backfired and needed contrite patching and repair. When I created Name, Claim and Reframe, I discovered that there was no way to be mindful without slowing down, stepping away, and observing with a new perspective. Reframing is like any daily practice: you have to take it one day at a time and keep exploring. Like the practices of Yoga or meditation, sometimes you see big shifts and feel like you have transcended to a higher frequency, and other times you slide backward feeling lost and confused. As long as you stay out of the self-judgment zone, even when you have a day that you wish you could take back, you are still advancing and learning. Cut yourself some slack, lean into humor, and know that your practice of reframing will last for a lifetime.

Reframing comes when we realign our thinking around a triggering situation and choose to respond with new ownership. It is the intentional act of using all of the elements that we have discussed in the previous chapters—the triggers of Naming, the proactive actions of Claiming, awareness around utilizing above the line masculine and feminine traits, all while leaning into our values and boundaries, and allowing ourselves more optimistic, strategic, and visionary thinking. In other words, while you may not be able to change what life throws your way, you can spin it in a more positive perspective that will better serve the boundaries of the new you.

When we set to Reframe our approach to an old problem, we do it by shifting our mindset. Now that you have Named and Claimed your triggers and are more comfortable sitting with your feelings, it's time to Reframe the whole situation and tackle the problem in a different way. You now have the foundation to be brave enough to understand the why of your past reactions and choose to take a softer, more intelligent path through life's adversities. This is the final step in the way of the Gentle Warrior.

Although the tests that you encounter will initially trigger your reactive ways of the past, they will also provide the opportunity to ultimately Name, Claim, and stand in your core values and boundaries. This is a time of exploration, curiosity, and rigorous compassion.

You may be put into new situations where you are asking the question, "How is this situation going to serve me?" Having freed yourself from old habits, you have the power of choice now while making new decisions. One day you may find yourself gifting time and generously offering helpful feedback, while another day you may decide that the best option is a firm but polite "No, thank you!" If the situation arises and you say a "*HELL NO!*" congratulations on the clarity of your boundaries and values. You have brought purpose to the Reframing of your mindset and have allowed your values to draw you closer to the essence of your essential self, your Gentle Warrior.

The Reframe stage is also about getting out of your own way using a metaphorical architecture that will support you as you navigate the inevitable shit-shows of life, someone else's circus, or a memory that triggers a time when you did not successfully stand in your best above the line power. My "Pre-Gentle-Warrior" self has a dusty trunk full of cringeworthy memories of defaults to territorial and confrontational tactics, usually when I was threatened or trying to mask my imperfections. In other words, I deferred to a below the line warrior's reaction, which is not a good look for any of us. Now instead of beating myself up about the past, I compassionately offer love to the younger, armored version of myself, reminding myself that transformation takes time, patience, and empathy. I also offer myself forgiveness when I am imperfect and give others the space to be so as well. Within these new containers grow the more expansive energies of compassion, grace, and self-sovereignty. We must offer ourselves the time and space for reflection so we can find the softer and more intentional way through.

Artist/poet/author Cleo Wade said, "Regret is focusing too much on decisions made when you were still learning." So, lighten up, surrender to the genius of your darkness, and consider yourself a brave explorer who is still in the process of learning how to show up as a more authentic version of themselves. When we choose to Name, Claim, and then Reframe with intention, we mindfully assess how we will engage with what we encounter outside of our energetic boundaries. By being truthful with ourselves, we not only start the healing process, but we also begin to build the architecture that will support who we are becoming.

Despite my creation of the Reframe step, I am the first one to admit that I have my own struggles trying to be mindful when I slide backwards. The atmosphere that offers me so much temptation to do so is my parents' home or as I call it, the "Hurricane House." For many of us, visiting a childhood home has a way of conjuring triggering, below the line, reactive energy. After hearing of how I had been unknowingly sucked into one of my parent's conflicts, a colleague asked me, "Why would you fly your helicopter into a hurricane?" meaning why haven't you created stronger boundaries for yourself with your parents? Her insight stopped me in my tracks. Who would be stupid enough to fly a helicopter into a hurricane? Me, that's who!

There has always been an uncertain turbulence that surrounds my parents' relationship. While they have been married for 63 years, the magic between them is steeped in a confrontational energy that continues to this day. Like a George Burns and Gracie Allen comedy routine, they lovingly banter, jab, and jeer at each other all day long, "Edward, stop eating those cookies!" or "Rosemary, what a stupid bridge bid, you're not paying attention!" Although their dark humor can be entertaining and very funny, my parents' mirthful jousting also has the power to pull me into my old reactive patterns of the past. To cope with the turbulent energy that surrounds their relationship, as I grew to adulthood, I took on the role of a first responder and became my family of origin's fixer: I rescued, facilitated, and advocated. This codependence impeded my ability to separate myself from the Hurricane House of my past, and the upgraded life that I had created with my husband and children. It was emotional rescue work that left me feeling invisible and undervalued with my energy resources almost always exhausted.

People in a hurricane do not care about who their rescuers are, they just want to be rescued. They want someone to receive their angst, soothe their worry, and create a safe space. However, where hurricanes are concerned, it is always best for helicopters (like me and maybe you) to stay away from them because it is simply unsafe to fly during a hurricane.

A big shift towards reframing my mindset towards the Hurricane House was to proactively create the terms of how I consciously engage when I leave the sanctuary of my land and enter my parents' house. The first step was to create energetic boundaries. This meant that I would not feel guilt or shame for disappointing someone. In other words, I practiced self-sovereignty by ensuring that my needs and the needs of my family's energy reserves come first. Stand firm and understand that there is always resistance when we redesign the terms of engagement. Although I call my parents almost every day, I limit my in-person visits to the days when I have the time and space to offer them my best. Checking in with my essential self helps me to preserve my energy supply so I manage everyone's expectations, including my own. I fly in and I fly out and then I go back to the sanctuary of my own land. Knowing that I have intentionally built a sanctum of sovereignty in the form a metaphorical land gives me the strength to ground in my own energetic boundaries before I attempt to visit foreign lands outside my borders.

We all have those places that we enter with trepidation. While some days may be calm and unremarkable, the weather patterns in foreign lands are out of our control, and we feel a sense of unease knowing that high winds could pick up at any moment. In order to survive in an environment that we perceive as tempestuous, we must first fortify ourselves with the provisions to weather whatever we encounter. We Name our triggers, Claim new energy, and Reframe by realigning our mindset so we can respond strategically. The idea that we have the power to intentionally "take our own weather" wherever we travel, helped me develop this concept into a tool that I use with clients: Build Your Land.

The goal of the Build Your Land exercise is that the architecture of the space (topography, weather, food, geography, cultural values, imports/exports, etc.) honors not only the energetic boundaries of the client's values, but the genius inside their personal shadow-version. I have had clients create tropical islands, French boutiques, enchanted forests, mountain retreats, and even a Mediterranean village. All that is required is that the land helps them integrate their core values so they can stand firm against the inevitable influences of the outside world.

BUILD YOUR LAND EXERCISE

- What core values and above-the-line M/F traits do you feature in your land?
- What mantras and/or core beliefs does this land symbolize for you?
- What do you "need to let go of" and/or "not require" when you visit this land?
- Reflect on your land's topography, climate, weather, food/culture, plant/animal life, music and exports. Expand on how each supports your core values and the resources available to you.
- Use descriptive language and visual aids to aid your inquiry.

Liv, a Human Resources coordinator for a large retailer, wanted to clarify her values so she could confidently guard the boundaries of "NO", not only professionally but in her personal life. Liv shared that at times, she had felt like a human doormat as she had allowed others to take advantage of her time, her talents, and her very generous heart. As we dove deeper, Liv learned that her Asian-American cultural values around being kind, generous, and non-confrontational now clashed significantly with the newfound values within the visionary land she hoped to create for her future. This realization helped Liv to Reframe her mindset around the power of saying not just "NO" but "Hell NO!" With new awareness, she began to take up more space and assert her authority when she noticed that her value boundaries had been threatened.

As Liv began to build her metaphorical peninsula, a non-negotiable was that her land be a sanctuary focused on inclusion, diversity, and belonging. Liv was dedicated to advocating and being a voice of inclusion for all, especially people of color. She enthusiastically included the themes of hope, acceptance, compassion, and diversity into her design. She envisioned a food court with multi-cultural culinary tastes, a reflective forest for introverts who needed a quiet retreat, and a meandering promenade that took in the mild climate and natural beauty of her land that mirrored her native San Francisco. Liv who had a passion for the San Francisco Giants, made sure that her land included a baseball stadium, an athlete's village, and a boutique that sold logo wear for all her favorite teams. In between sessions, Liv created a map visual of her sanctuary using drawings and descriptive wording that reflected the metaphorical structure of who she was becoming: "I now believe that I am strong and worthy. Saying no is not selfish, it helps me Reframe who I have become. My land is where I go when the energy suckers or naysayers tread on my value boundaries."

Liv played the 2018 Kasey Musgraves' song, "Rainbow" to upgrade the energy she hoped to embody and carried the themes of diversity and inclusion forward onto her website, a side passion project she had launched as a Bay Area Sports Influencer. Liv's land became a place of refuge when she needed to get in touch with the woman she was becoming.

Like the mini values assessments that I outlined in Chapter Five, metaphorical retreats can serve as a foundational inquiry to help clients define and anchor in the "why" behind their value boundaries. A close cousin of this concept is vision boarding, using descriptive words, graphics, and photos to map out clear intentions and expectations for the future. Many clients come to coaching having mapped out what they want in life, and our work together can absolutely serve as a source of stability that helps them draft and carry out their plans. Yet there are times when emotional attachments to value-based visions and outcomes can also limit our ability to objectively align with these very same goals,

especially when we are faced with unexpected plot twists that trap us into an old way of thinking.

"Life is a story that unfolds between a beginning we can no longer remember and an end we know nothing about."

—UNKNOWN

Don't cling too tightly to one path as the universe often presents options, opportunities and routes that may look very different than the blueprint you so carefully drafted. While we can most certainly use our masculine drive to achieve goals, we must blend it with our feminine ingenuity, so that we will not miss the sparkly diamond gifts that are often hidden in the rough patches along the path.

Kaitlyn had razor focused expectations for herself and her imminent future. She wanted a fresh start in New York City and had narrowed her job search accordingly. Kaitlyn had become frustrated in her role as a junior designer at a boutique interior architecture firm located in San Francisco. Kaitlyn's mentality was simple, New York or bust! This expansive vision included a larger interiors firm where she could hone her skills as a designer, expand her portfolio, and increase her salary and benefits. Yet, as COVID-19 shelter in place orders descended upon the world, Kaitlyn felt trapped, fearing she had lost sight of her New York dreams. Her inability to think outside the box meant that pessimism was now knocking at her front door, and she needed help to Reframe her approach.

She arrived at our session distraught and confused. A recruiter had tapped her for a higher paying design role at a bigger, more influential firm, but Kaitlyn was conflicted, as this larger role was also located in San Francisco. This unexpected plot twist was a fly in the ointment for

Kaitlyn who was wary of the opportunity because it clashed with her carefully curated vision of the future. She reluctantly interviewed for the position and, despite her quiet reservation, had received an enticing verbal offer from the principle of the firm. Instead of celebrating, Kaitlyn was downcast and allowed her expectations to take the lead in her thinking:

"I'm so disappointed in myself." she moaned. "Three years ago, I would have jumped at the chance to interview with this firm. Even though it is a great job and good money, I feel like I'm giving up on my dreams if I don't hold out for New York. What if I hate it and am stuck living someone else's dream instead of my own?"

Instead of taking pleasure in the surprising circumstances that had been laid out before her, Kaitlyn mourned for the shiny option she had built in her dreams. Unsure of how to Claim her next steps, she had hindered her creativity and squelched her resourcefulness to Reframe the situation. The path out of an unexpected outcome is not pessimism. If we can Reframe the optimism of what could be, instead of what isn't, we free ourselves from the restraints of the narrow targets we have set and open our hearts to a wider variety of possible outcomes.

"Let's Reframe this surprise option, Kaitlyn. What if you couldn't fail?" I asked her, "What if this job is more about what you have to learn so you are ready when a New York opportunity presents itself? Truthfully, what is the worst thing that could happen if you trust yourself and boldly take the job?" I posed.

"The worse thing is that I hate it and have to find another job," she answered.

"Can you live with that outcome?" I countered.

"Yes . . . I can. Also this job offer has shown me that I am a valuable commodity and firms are looking to hire people with my unique skill set" she said truthfully.

"Ok, dream with me . . . What is the best thing that might happen if you take this job?" I proposed.

"The best thing is that I love the job, earn more money and gain a new skills that will get me one step closer to my dream of living in New York," she said as a calmer and wiser version of herself.

"How can you Reframe your thinking around this opportunity?" I asked Kaitlyn.

"That maybe my next move is looking a little different than I thought it would. That there is learning in everything, and that I really can't lose by taking this job and staying in San Francisco. Besides, the increased salary means I can now afford to live on my own without roommates," she laughed.

The next day, Kaitlyn texted: "I got the formal offer and for more money than I expected. The recruiter told me that I am the Rolls Royce that they have been looking for. It feels so good to be seen and paid what I am worth. I have decided to leap with the intent to learn!" she said, her optimism present and accounted for.

Not only had Kaitlyn Reframed her thinking about the positive aspects of an unanticipated outcome, but she also gave herself permission to feel the warmth of her own light. "I had no idea that anyone would want to hire me this badly. It feels so good to be valued and wanted," she said, "I am so excited for this new beginning." After our session, Kaitlyn took great joy in curating a new vision board with her Reframed dreams for the future.

The further we distance ourselves from the exactness of our expectations, the more exhilarating our life will become. Think of unexpected outcomes as delicious ambiguity. Though a situation may not correspond to our initial wants, needs, or goals, when we Reframe "what might be possible," instead of what isn't, we receive the power of life's unexpected blessings.

Reframing Criticism and Feedback

Many of us have over-compensated in our actions to bypass criticism. My childhood home was flooded with witty critiques, and to avoid them, I conscientiously worked to complete tasks efficiently before my father discovered where I had missed the mark. One Saturday afternoon as I settled down to enjoy a toasted cheese sandwich for lunch, he stormed into the house and yelled at me for a chore I had left undone. As I ran outside to complete the neglected task, he settled down and ate my lunch. My mother looked at my father and said half-jokingly, "First you yell at her and then you have the nerve to eat her lunch."

My takeaway from these kinds of experiences was a sincere effort to cover all my bases by "overdoing" so I would never get caught messing up. Although I used both masculine, above and below the line behaviors to be sure that I did not leave a single stone unturned, I also used my feminine below the line reactions of people pleasing and avoidance. Obviously, this is not any way for a fallible human to go through life and I often failed. While today I am far enough away enough to understand that my father's lunch poaching was consistent with his short-tempered parenting style, his redirects often inhibited my integrity and chipped away at my confidence. He was notoriously impatient with both of my brothers and me, expecting us to know how to do things without ever teaching us the rules. As backwards as it sounds, when we erred, he used criticism to teach us what he wanted us to learn. At the end of one summer, to impress him with my progressive thinking, I wisely filled the speed boat's gas tank before putting it back on the trailer for the winter storage. My father's critique: "That was a stupid thing to do, Andrea, we never put the boat into storage with a full gas tank. What were you thinking?"

The good news is that I learned how to do things by messing up first and never made the same mistake again. The bad news is that no matter how hard I tried to avoid criticism, it was inevitable. Reframing my negative association with feedback began by leaning into curiosity not only about how to receive it gracefully, but more importantly, how to then use it strategically to my advantage.

The root word for criticism, critic, originates from the Latin word, "criticus", which means a judge, censor, or specifically a grammarian who evaluates literary work. If authors were afraid of critics, no books would ever be written, including this one. We deem critics skilled at judging the merit of things, and we rely on them to provide helpful commentary on everything from the best cars to buy, to the next binge-worthy series on Netflix. I read critical reviews with great interest, but I have quite the opposite reaction when I encounter a critical comment about something that I have created.

While criticism is focused on what we didn't do right in the past, feedback is more nuanced with suggestions about how we might improve and Reframe our mindset for the future. I was bewildered in my first job performance review when my boss gave me positive feedback and then Reframed it by gifting me ideas to further improve my skill. It was criticism disguised in a friendly and Reframed feedback package. My superior's feedback didn't make me feel bad, in fact his review capitalized on my strengths and gave me things to strive for in the future. Because of my criticism infused childhood, it is not surprising that I am suspicious of feedback. I wish I had made the distinction between the two types of feedback earlier in my life, as I often misconstrued all forms of feedback as criticism, or ways that I had failed. If we are to adopt the way of the Gentle Warrior, receiving evaluations of any sort becomes a delicate dance in mindfully Reframing what to call in and what to cast out.

So how do we Reframe criticism and feedback in a Gentle Warrior way? We first remove ourselves from the expectations of others. While it may be unconscious, feedback can easily land on us like criticism, triggering past wounds and their tag-a-long false identities. Suddenly, like clockwork, we feel pinched as unhealthy feelings of failure rush in and block our ability to see the way out of the limiting beliefs we have about ourselves. If we can learn to accept feedback graciously, we avoid the wall of self-doubt that blocks our productive and creative flow.

I considered myself a Gentle Warrior when I began to write this book. I had a confidence about who I had been as an educator and a coach, but at the same time I was nervous about my abilities as an author. As I Named a desire to take up more space as a thought leader, I was also Claiming a new path within the uncertain norms of the book writing process. I had no idea how to proceed or what roadblocks I might encounter. And worse, I had never experienced the scrutiny of allowing someone to teach me by editing my writing. Meeting with my editor was initially excruciating, as I likened it to memories of my father punishing me for being wrong. Instead of being an explorer, open to all the ways that my editor was making my writing shine brighter, I only saw all the ways my writing had failed. I led with my ego rather than getting curious about what was possible and how I might begin to grow as a writer. As I hunkered down in the pit of my shadow-version of self, I blocked all creative flow and new perspectives, welcoming in my inner critic's rueful regrets. Self-loathing from perceived ineptitude is like hiding in a dark cave with your eyes and ears closed. You will never find your way out unless you get curious and look for the light within the darkness.

When it dawned on me that I had taken the action to hire a skilled editor that could guide me through the writing process and that I was, in fact, smart enough to enlist this kind of support so I could expand and learn, I leaned into the edits as feedback and collaboration versus criticism or evidence that I wasn't worthy to author a book.

When we Reframe and lean into our imperfections, we welcome in learning, adaptation, and the modifications we may have never considered. We are open to collaboration, and benefit from the skills of others as they in turn gain new perspectives from our point of view. Seeking another's critique creates the chance for us to become better. Plus, it is in the exploration of the rough edges, counterintuitive routes, and boldly broken rules that make our work provocative, unique, and unforgettable. I have learned that it is in the raw fragility of our fears and most painful emotions that that we receive the genius inside the shadow-version of ourselves. It is when we reveal our imperfections and struggles that we become more relatable and accessible to others, especially those we hope to impress.

The root of the word education is the Latin word, "educare" meaning to draw forth from within or to lead out. Instead of criticism, your mentors are generously drawing out the invaluable strengths that they see emerging from within. When someone offers feedback, shift, and sort it, calling in only the precious gems that will serve you. Thank them gratefully and then quietly cast out the parts that do not match where you are going.

In her 2015 best-selling book, *Play Big*, author Tara Mohr presents valuable insights into how to "unhook" yourself from both praise or criticism, and more effectively shape feedback to match your goals and visions for the future. Mohr explains that the act of "unhooking" is consciously distancing yourself from the immediate emotional response—the "fight or flight" urge or what I call the Naming step. Mohr's work, especially around how to navigate the criticism that matches up with the limiting beliefs we hold about ourselves, significantly impacted my perspectives and helped to shape the strategies I present here for Reframing feedback.

Still, Reframing can get muddled when we mix it with money, causing us to believe that the way someone compensates us is feedback about the value we are offering. Often our beliefs around money start with our family of origin and if we are to truly stand firm in our worth, we must have a clear understanding of not only our core value system, but the value we are being paid to offer. When we take on a wounded mindset, feeling less than worthy, money wise, we are not aligned with our essential selves, and this weakens our energetic boundaries.

When I started my coaching practice, I struggled to stand firmly in a competitive hourly rate. I felt unworthy because I was earning my hours, honing my skills and had not yet been officially certified through the International Coaching Federation. I had not Claimed myself as a viable coach and my wishy-washy vagueness made me a victim when a potential client complained my fee was too high. Instead of admitting (or Claiming) that she did not possess the energy frequency of someone who valued the service I was offering, I hedged, giving her a cheaper rate so I could win the sale. I immediately regretted my decision as she repeatedly no showed for our sessions and ignored my invoices. I was further humiliated when I was forced to chase her down with a stream of overdue notices for sessions that she had received but not paid for. Because I accepted a lower standard of pay, she mirrored it by showing up with a lower standard of respect which undercut my confidence and professionalism. Her inferior energy frequency made me feel resentful, and I dreaded our sessions because the energy around them clashed with my values and the service I wanted to give my clients. Abigail, a trusted mentor and colleague offered me this advice, "Don't undervalue your services or clients will too. You are too powerful a coach to allow this kind of disrespect, Andrea. You do have the power to fire a client!"

Her wise counsel helped me to Reframe not only how I saw myself, but also my mindset around giving myself the power to choose who I coach. The way a person shows up does not give feedback about you, it only gives feedback about that person. This client's unwillingness to pay a fair market price for my services told me everything I needed to understand about her and what she valued. The Reframe: her behavior reflected nothing about my impact as a coach, yet I had allowed her actions to hinder the energetic boundaries of my coaching practice. To realign with my core values, I Claimed an action, I fired the client. Cutting this client loose felt like an act of freedom and helped me to stand confidently in my growing skill as a coach. It also prompted me to create the necessary policies and procedures so that I could feel valued, professional, and worthy, especially to myself.

If we open our hearts to dissonant experiences, they can help us to Name what we can't be with, Claim the learning within the snafu and then Reframe our new mindset accordingly. In other words, interesting errors, mistakes, and blunders often birth the most fabulous recoveries. Next time a lower energy type tromps your integrity, lean into humility, and realign with your core values. Maybe this is the universe gifting you a much-needed energetic boundary check.

Sometimes the feedback we receive has nothing to do with us and is completely out of our control. Before we allow an offhand remark or someone else's bad behavior to get our inner critic chattering, stop, step away and gather the facts. The reason that negative feedback stings is because it reinforces the ideals that are contained in the shadow-versions of who we are.

"... often what feels like a problem with painful criticism
is really a problem with what we believe about ourselves."

—TARA MOHR, *Playing Big*

If we can focus on where the self-limiting belief (or maybe even the core wound) originates, it makes it easier to Name, Claim and Reframe a new, updated belief that better matches the person we hope to become. Not everyone plays nice and sometimes it can be as simple as: "This person doesn't share my values and I need to cut my loses and move on."

Now that I have gotten more comfortable with feedback, I try to curate a targeted learning goal when I approach others for their ideas. It helps me to balance their opinions with the objectives I have for myself. It's like getting a feedback booster, I create a plan of how I will use the feedback to become more skilled and informed. When I do a workshop, I always ask participants for feedback in a structured container that I have created and, by not allowing an open forum, I control how I take it in the feedback. Their remarks are an informative assessment of how my content was received, and points me towards places I might need modifications. The best part about asking for feedback is that it highlights areas I might not have considered. New perspectives can lead to innovation or opportunity. Being strategic in seeking feedback that targets specific areas is a beautiful way to expand your thinking, toughen up your once thin skin and find the gift within the offering. This principle can be applied to everything from a new podcast idea to planning a bird watching trip to Costa Rica. Next time you get stung by feedback, separate your ego from bad bits so you can call in the good parts that better match the upgraded frequency of you.

REFRAMING FEEDBACK EXERCISE

Any form of feedback only gives you information about the individual providing the feedback; i.e., *What they value*. Another person's opinion doesn't tell you anything essential about you.

It's not about you. Think about the last time you received feedback, either positive or negative. What, if anything, does the feedback tell you about the core values of the person that gave you the feedback?

Call-in and cast-off. CALL-IN only the pieces of the feedback that match your goals for the future. CAST-OFF the pieces of feedback that do not support your newly reframed mindset.

Name the sting. When feedback feels more like a "criticism sting", slow down and reflect on how the feedback mirrors a core wound, a false identity, or a limiting belief.

- NAME the core wound, false identity, or limiting belief.
- CLAIM your emotions by separating your ego from the facts around the feedback. What action could be taken so you can feel better?
- REFRAME your below-the-line thinking with a new perspective that will support an above-the-line mindset going forward.

Gather the facts. Separate your ego from the feedback by gathering the facts about the situation, both positive and negative. Break it down so you can separate yourself further from the sting by interpreting the reality of the situation.

- List the facts and look at the situation logically. Name and Claim the evidence.
- What story is your inner critic spinning? Call out the voice and send it away.

Target your reframe. Always CLAIM a target objective when you ask for feedback so you can Reframe critiques to match your goals for learning.

- What do I hope to learn here?
- What parts of this feedback can I CALL-IN?
- Which parts do I need to CAST-OUT?
- What interesting perspectives might help expand my thinking?

Navigating Compliments

Receiving is feminine and there is a bona fide grace to accepting compliments. Whether it be a kind word about your appearance or a colleague praising a job well done, we often struggle to accept positive acknowledgments. Some of us even bat them away suspiciously, like skilled goalies, never allowing ourselves the opportunity to soak in the praise. What is it about compliments that make us so uncomfortable?

I am a self-proclaimed blocker of praise, wary of its sincerity and quick to insert a self-deprecating comment to further disprove the recognition. I either don't process the compliment or I don't believe it. Another trick I use is to dodge flattery altogether—like a tennis player,

I lob a solid forehand back over the net, changing the focus to the other person. One day, after a colleague had kindly complimented me, he caught me in the act of dodging his praise, "Andrea, please take in what I just said. Hear it and stand in it. You are worthy of praise."

He was right and, in that moment when I let his generous offering land upon me, like a joyous sprinkle of confetti. It felt so very wonderful to be complimented and his earnest observation got me thinking about my struggle to receive praise. My mother, who collects compliments like cherished trophies, has always said, "When someone is giving you a compliment, NEVER interrupt." Praise seems to fuel her, and she receives it with both gratitude and joy. When we were growing up, she served as our family's compliment ambassador, receiving compliments on behalf of her children, and then passing them along to us like little SweeTarts. Maybe that's why I was suspicious of them, they were hand-me-downs and didn't really feel like I owned them: "Mrs. So-So thinks you're darling." What does "darling" even mean and how am I supposed to use this information going forward? I was looking for more detailed and focused input, or something that might point me towards either affirmation or improvement. What I didn't know then was that I needed a Reframe on how to gracefully accept and navigate praise when I was lucky enough to receive it.

Tanya Geisler, Imposter Complex expert and the brilliant thought leader behind "Your Impeccable Impact" gave me this advice around acknowledgment: "If the acknowledgment you are receiving is not meeting you where you need to be met, use the praise as an opportunity to ask for what you need."

In other words: Are there specific nuances you can ask the giver of the praise to address that will better match the feedback you are looking to receive?

But there can be delicate nuances to these inquiries as Tanya elaborates, "For example, if someone praises me for my power and I want them to see my tenderness, it might be inappropriate for me to expect them to see my tenderness, because (as I reflect), the giver of the praise may have only witnessed my power. As I receive their kind praise, I might say 'Thank you for seeing my power, but I am also hoping that you experienced my tenderness within it.'"

By strategically separating yourself from the limiting beliefs around the acknowledgment, you do have the power to ask for the specific and targeted feedback that you are seeking. Tanya stresses that although there is great vulnerability in asking for what you need, we must also be discriminatory about who we invite into these kinds of exchanges, a trusted colleague, or friend can be a wonderful sounding board, whereas clarification may not be appropriate with a stranger who approaches you at the end of a keynote. In other words, carefully chose the thought partners you welcome into the sifting and sorting of acknowledgments. Tanya's wise counsel, like Tara Mohr's work around all forms feedback and criticism has helped me to Reframe and shapeshift old stories into revised perspectives that have truly helped me Reframe my tendency towards below the line thinking.

One day, an acquaintance approached me in the grocery store, sharing how much she loved receiving my monthly newsletter. "I love the topics you are writing about, Andrea. I actually printed out February's theme and have placed it on my desk for reference" she gushed.

I thanked her but I didn't believe her for a minute, which is ludicrous because, why would this woman, who hardy knew me, lie? In fact, she had even provided me with the specifics about what she liked in my newsletter. Still the shadow-version of myself was skeptical, and I hesitated to allow her accolades to soak in, pondering to myself: "Maybe her remarks teetered towards patronizing because she feels sorry for me and wants to be kind?"

My old pattern had returned, swiftly deflecting praise by swatting it away. But my Gentle Warrior within got curious and as I drove home, I began the process of Reframing her praise with a bit more reflection: "Why am I so uncomfortable accepting this praise?" As I Named the imposter syndrome through that question, I Claimed it by giving myself permission to acknowledge the compliment, and then went on to Reframe the feedback by admitting that I had written a very good piece. I owned it, giving myself a moment to stand in my own light. By noticing the origin of my negative belief, I updated it with a more compassionate and empowering Reframe that fit who I was becoming, a thought leader and writer. When I got home, I further Reframed my thinking. This compliment had provided information about how my writing was landing with the demographic I had targeted. I welcomed in gratitude for all those who read and valued what I was writing. I also decided to separate my ego even further from the feedback by using it to home in on my target audience. This was important because there is always a flip side to feedback. When someone chooses to unsubscribe from my newsletter, it provides data about who was NOT interested in what I have to say. When it comes to the folks who are not part of your cheering section, don't let your ego get too attached. Instead, limit your precious energy only to those who value your magnificence. I could have spent a long time blindly spinning my wheels about my doubt over the woman's compliment, but instead, during my short car ride home I had gifted myself a mindful Reframe and shifted my mindset to a higher frequency!

Tricia Bolender, my mentor coach, and a trusted colleague, says that receiving a legitimate compliment is something of an art form, or rather a three-part process:

- We must first be present enough to allow the accolade a safe place to land.
- We must then accept it with gratitude.
- Finally, we must celebrate the sensation of awe that we feel when we are truly seen, heard, and acknowledged.

Tell a child under five that you are proud of them and watch their response. Children embody the art of receiving with a synergy of grace, joy, and elation. They let it land and then gratefully celebrate their own light. There is a poise to receiving, and it means that you accept with gratitude another's Offe ring and agree to celebrate yourself. Yet most of us are uncomfortable receiving praise. My theory is that many of us discount the giver's compliment so that we won't outshine them with our own light. We struggle to stand in our own magnificence because we are fearful that if we openly acknowledge our radiance, people will not want to be part of our trusted posse. We think that shifting the frequency of the flattery to the other person will make us more likable. You play "compliment tennis" by thanking them quickly and then countering back, "But where did you get your bag? It's so much nicer than mine!"

Conversely, when we are called out for our gifts and talents, it can also conjure an unwelcome obligation to stand up and meet the praise. We might feel resentful or put upon that in receiving the compliment, we will have to match it by DOING something or risk being seen as sorely inadequate. Whatever is holding you back, Name and Claim so you can Reframe the praise in a way that will serve what you need in that specific moment.

Tricia, who knows that receiving compliments with grace is one of my weaker areas, coaxed me to practice "the art of receiving" on a Zoom call when she asked three other women to award me compliments. Although I was allowed to say a simple "thank you" to each show of praise, my only job was to sit and receive. It was an out of body experience for me; being presence and allowing each compliment a safe place to land, the gratitude of connection with others while allowing myself permission to celebrate the radiance I was projecting out into the world. These women, many who I did not know well, saw my truths, my light and my inner beauty and told me so. At first, I tried to capture the incredible things they were saying and then I stopped and just let it rain down upon it me. I found myself being warmed from the inside out. You are safe, you are loved, you are whole, and you are holy.

When someone offers you praise, stop, and allow the generous observation to sink in. This is you shining your light out into the world and receiving acknowledgment of your work as a Gentle Warrior. The sensation of awe to be seen, recognized, and even admired. All that is needed in return is a simple, "Thank you." Think about the qualities you admire in others and know that they exist in you as well. Embracing recognition and endorsement is proof that others see the gifts that you have brought into the world. It is this symbiotic exchange that promotes above the line generosity, receptiveness, and community.

> "Life is an echo. What you send out, comes back. What you sow, you reap. What you give, you get. What you see in others, exists in you."
>
> —ZIG ZIGLAR

There can also be a dark side to praise as it has a way of soothing our insecurities and feelings of inadequacy. If you feel wobbly about something that you've done, asking for reassurance can shore up your deficient feelings. Yes, there are times when "roughly right" is all that is required but be honest with yourself. A flawed effort followed by honest feedback gives you the opportunity to glean new insight, pivot your strategy, or improve your approach. We can't use the feeling of false perfection as a cover for our fear of getting an earnest critique, and faux praise is not going to support a strong Gentle Warrior stance. If we are only asking for feedback to salve a regret that we have, then we are giving up our power and sense of worthiness to another's opinion. When we are willing to be honest about an imperfect effort, we force ourselves to realize the only thing holding us back is our fear, and with a Gentle Warrior Reframe, we can lean into the learning.

Reframing Compliments

When receiving a compliment:

- Provide the praise a safe place to land by saying a simple, "Thank you!"
- Receive the praise by allowing the awe of gratitude to flow over you.
- Celebrate yourself for shining your light out into the world.

Compliments give us insight into the person giving the feedback. Think about the last time you received praise for something:

- What might the compliment tell you about this person's values or perceptions of the world?
- How might I use this praise to celebrate myself and my goals for the future?
- Are there specific nuances that you can ask the giver of the praise to address that better match the feedback you are looking to receive?

- **NAME** any limiting belief within the praise that might be rubbing up against a past core wound or a false identity.
- **CLAIM** your magnificence. What is this praise telling you about the gifts that you bring to the world?
- **REFRAME** by realigning your mindset with new ownership. Cast-out any below-the-line thinking and Call-in a refreshed above-the-line perspective.

All of this takes practice, like building a muscle, but if you lighten up and learn to approach feedback, criticism, and compliments with an open heart, you can harvest information, like a person's tastes, norms, expectations, etc. Once you have called in what will serve you, you have the freedom to let the rest of it go. When we can separate our ego from the fear of the evaluation and get curious about what the feedback is providing, we transform what was once another person's opinion into a mindful Reframe that will enhance our brilliance and our vision for the future.

As you embody the energy and actions of a Gentle Warrior, be assured that you will continue to negotiate and renegotiate the Reframe step. While some of your Reframes will be clear and easy to navigate, others will take more care, reflection, and honest assessment. I too am still evolving into a woman who is "closer" to her essential self, but Naming, Claiming and Reframing has allowed me to lighten up and realize that other people's opinions and patronizing praise do not serve my integrity and are best discarded. As you stand more confidently in who you are, you will have more gratitude towards those who were kind enough to provide helpful guidance as well as the poise to gracefully sidestep someone's unsolicited point of view. When we thoughtfully sort through and extract the hidden gems that will help us to grow, it's easier to cast out the fragments that do not.

Take a deep breath and congratulate yourself, you are completely primed and prepped with all the tools to Name, Claim and Reframe yourself into a Gentle Warrior. Before we dive into the world at large and turn theory into practice, let's do a quick overview of the system.

The Gentle Warrior's Toolbox

Name: Gain Awareness by Naming Your Pain Point:

- What can't you "be with" or tolerate about the situation?
- What emotions/feelings/core-wound have might have been triggered by the situation?
- What value boundary has been violated?

*Beware of your inner critic's fears. Reassure the voice and send it away so you can be present with your essential self.

Claim: Move Forward by Claiming New Energy:

- Try to separate your ego from the situation so you can look at the facts.
- What about your actions caused the other person to react negatively?
- What action could be taken to move forward and feel better?

*Use the Masculine/Feminine chart on page 24 to identify an above-the-line action.

Reframe: Realign Your Perspective and Respond with New Ownership:

- Create a mindset that encourages optimistic, strategic, or visionary thinking.
- List the ways your response/action might better serve the boundaries of the new you.
- Detach from your below-the-line actions of the past and lead with new aligned self-confidence.

Theory into Practice Case Study

THE NAME: When one of the employees that reported directly to her, consistently failed to disregard the clear deadlines she had set and ignored her gentle reminders, Claire Named her feelings of anger which threatened her core value boundaries of respect, partnership, and accomplishment. The naming step helped Claire to admit that she felt resentful and disrespected which had caused her to dip below the line with controlling, codependent, and resentful reactions.

THE CLAIM: Claire chose the action of providing direct and specific feedback to her subordinate. Not only did she give him an honest assessment of his less than stellar performance, but Claire also outlined her expectations for him going forward and provided suggestions on how he might improve the core skills need to do his job. In separating her ego from the situation, Claire detached herself from her past tendency to control outcomes, "I realize that his inability to meet the mark had nothing to do with me or my ability to do my job."

THE REFRAME: Detaching herself from her employee's poor attitude and performance helped Claire to honor her own integrity as a leader. In stepping away, she was able to use altruistic vision to create a structured set of expectations for herself and those she hoped to influence.

While some situations can be easily resolved, others take more patience and scrutiny as the tentacles of emotion and the core wounds within them run deeper. Celebrate the wins and don't despair over the murkier waters. Lean into the learning and know that despite the bruises you might receive, a Gentle Warrior always emerges enlightened, at peace, and above the line.

Now let's walk through some of our more tenuous circumstances and practice these tools. Scenarios with our family and work life provide ample opportunities to practice Name, Claim and Reframe. When you are in the bloody battle, it's easy to lose composure and drop below the line. As I have learned in my own life, understanding how to integrate theory into practice is imperative before we muddy the waters with even trickier situations.

CHAPTER SEVEN

Name, Claim & Reframe

FAMILY

WHILE ONE CAN UNDERSTAND THE CONCEPTS OF NAME, Claim and Reframe, the mastery of integration is a lifetime practice, especially when it comes to those in your inner orbit, and the core triggers of family. As I discussed the Naming of family energy in Chapter Three (Name), we are now practicing Naming our experiences with these folks. I am speaking here about the people in our family, our spouses, children, extended family, and in-laws. Face it, when you fall in love and marry, not only do you inherit each other's parents, you welcome in new siblings, their spouses, their offspring and a limitless potential for chaos and conflict. These people are supposed to know all about you and love you anyway, but there will be pushback as you change the ways you want to be viewed by the whole motley package. For the most part, you can't get rid of your family of origin, and if we move to Reframe circumstances in a more positive light, this circle will most certainly provide the best opportunity for practicing the mindful Reframe.

My family have continued to gift me with a plethora of muddy messes to both assess and recalibrate in pursuit of a more Gentle Warrior response. As I discussed in Chapter Four, you have Claimed and upgraded your frequency, and the people closest to you are going to notice, react, and want to push you right back to the lower frequency of your past. The change they see in you indicates that the rules of the game have been altered, and that scares the hell out of them. You are the facilitator to all those in your familial orbit (yourself, your aging parents, and your children) and although we might have conflicting reactions in our heads as well as in our hearts, honoring the integrity of these relationships takes a combination of maturity, self-sovereignty, and a practiced mastery of the Name, Claim and Reframe management system.

Once you get the family part of your life centered and flowing, you can then move on to managing the people in your outer orbit—your social circle, your work environment, and all the eclectic personalities that you will encounter in the real world.

Aging Parents

If you can handle a contentious scrimmage with your mother, I propose that you can mostly likely handle any nosy neighbor that darkens your doorway. Your aging parents are doing the best they can. When the road gets rough, I remind myself of this point of view. My world and external responsibilities have expanded, while concurrently my geriatric parents' world has shrunk. Their friends are dying, their health is declining, and they need my love, attention, patience, and counsel.

Instead of dropping your apprehensive five-year-old off at kindergarten, you are pleading with your frustrated father who threatens to leave his hospital room before he has been officially discharged. Although you know that the nurse will eventually arrive with his release papers, you are torn between soothing his angry impatience and doing what is responsible. You are exhausted and desperate for a quick and peaceful resolution. You reluctantly acquiesce to your father's temper tantrum and then find yourself assisting his getaway wheelchair down the corridor and into the hospital elevator. This was MY sudden awakening that caused me (to feel) a triage of unclear identities, "Am I the child? Am I the parent? Or am I the unpaid consultant?" Propelled by love and motivated by an innate obligation, your role has shifted significantly. You are now *parenting* your parents.

One of my dearest college friends, Cathy, embodied compassionate grace after her mother, Edie, contracted Scabies and Cathy found herself temporarily housing her 85-year-old, dazed and confused mother in their home. Scabies (a contagious, intensely itchy skin condition caused by a tiny, burrowing mite called *Sarcoptes scabiei* who sets up shop in the outer layers of human skin) is common in nursing homes and spread by direct, prolonged, skin-to-skin contact. A 24-hour a day job, Cathy bravely dug in, moving her mother into their guest room and assuming all aspects of her mother's care. This included a specialized diet, bathing, and treating the highly transmittable rash on her mother's body. Not surprisingly, Cathy and her which also husband also contracted the intensely itchy skin rash.

"Once she settled in, my mother was so happy to be with us. I found myself nurturing her as she had once nurtured me," Cathy reflected. "But it's too much and I'm researching assisted living facilities that my mom can afford."

The situation was even more remarkable as for most of Cathy's life, Edie had displayed erratic, unreasonable, and downright mean behavior towards her daughter. Their strained and contentious relationship had improved in recent years when Edie had finally been diagnosed with a personality and mood disorder. Cathy had worked tirelessly with doctors to diagnose and fine tune her mother's treatment, so they could stabilize her outbursts and find medication that addressed the issue. The ordeal had pulled Cathy more towards forgiveness and acceptance, Reframing her mindset as she became Edie's compassionate caretaker and staunch advocate.

Each time we spoke, Cathy infused this earlier Reframe with a combination of humor for the obscurity of the situation (soothing a confused grandmother with mites in her hair) and a fierce familial love for her mother's well-being—mind, body, and soul. This Reframe transformed Cathy's once resentful mindset into one that called in devotion, resourcefulness, and gratitude for the opportunity to connect with her now sweet and docile mother on a deeper emotional level.

A year later, after her mother, Edie, died peacefully in the beautiful convalescent placement that Cathy had lovingly chosen for her, Cathy reflected, "Even though the scabies ordeal was disgusting, it gave me the opportunity to forgive the crazy parts of my mother's past. She and I shared an incredible intimacy at the end of her life and my mother was sweet, kind and very grateful. I have no regrets; my mother left this world knowing how much I loved her, and I'd do it all again."

Although the borders of Cathy's energetic boundaries were most certainly strained during her mother's unexpected visit, Cathy never lost sight of Naming the why behind her actions as she Claimed the values that drove them. When we take the time to Reframe our mindset around a strained or conflicted relationship, we allow ourselves to see the good that has come from it. "When my mom was healthy, she was a devoted parent," Cathy explained. "I am choosing to remember the good things that my mother taught us. I know how much she loved me because she told me at the end of her life. Working so closely with her doctors these past few years, I understand now how sick my mother was when we were young and how she must have struggled to keep it all together for me and my brother."

In becoming her mother's advocate, Cathy was able to Reframe and update her mindset, by casting out the painful memories of the past, a necessary step in the process that ultimately forged the relationship with her mother she had longed for most of her life.

Achieving a balanced level of self-sovereignty while parenting parents can be hugely difficult to navigate, especially when one is dealing with dementia. While we can intellectualize why our parent now behaves more like a bratty toddler, we are still human and struggle to look beyond their mental incapacity. If we are to rise above the line, we must Name and accept the way the insults or egregious actions feel on impact.

Dayna came to our session one day in tears. She Named both an energetic boundary intrusion and the deep hurt that she felt when her father-in-law accusingly called her a "selfish gold digger." The insult was unfounded and ill-fitting as in the past year, Dayna had selflessly spent her weekends coordinating his grocery shopping, meal prep, and the 24-hour care providers that supported her father-in-law. In fact, Dayna had generously practiced ongoing support towards her husband's parents her entire married life. She invited them to dinner every Sunday, took her mother-in-law grocery shopping and accompanied her father-in-law to medical appointments. While Dayna understood that her father-in-law's outburst was fueled more by dementia than ill intent, his name-calling still felt like a punch to the stomach. The ugly false identity had hooked her unfairly and Dayna needed to Claim the why of her values to shore up this rather unforeseen boundary violation. As we talked more, Dayna began to detach her ego from the situation as she reflected on the confusion and health issues that had plagued and frustrated her father-in-law since his wife's passing. From the perspective of a Gentle Warrior, and safely tapping into an above the line feminine response, Dayna could see that he was intensely lonely and had lashed out at her only to gain some semblance of control.

"He has always treated me like an adopted daughter more than a daughter-in-law, and I sense his behavior was his way of reminding me that he was still in charge of his life," as Dayna spoke these words, her eyes filled with tears. The hurt gave way to sadness for his condition.

The Reframe began when Dayna called in compassion and love, not only for her father-in-law but for herself. His time was limited, and the family needed to adjust his care. The incident was also a signal that Dayna needed to step away from the frontline. Although she continued to quietly support her father-in-law behind the scenes, Dayna asked her husband to handle all interpersonal exchanges with his father going forward. When she Reframed her approach by focusing on forgiveness, she was able to rise above the muck of an ugly moment, heal her heart and dance in the more advanced and graceful frequency of herself and her energetic boundaries.

Even when our parents are gone, we can never truly escape the dynamics of our family of origin. Most of us can coast along with Claiming our energy and boundaries, but when conflict kicks up, it can be a different game. Adult sibling rivalry is alive and well in most families, and our brothers and sisters are especially skilled at triggering our boundaries when it comes to money and property. When values that were never aligned suddenly collide, resentment builds, and conflict is inevitable. A perfect time for the Gentle Warrior to assess how to Claim a higher frequency action. After her 98-year-old mother passed, Brit's older sister went against their mother's wishes and bestowed all the family jewelry to herself and her three grown daughters. Instead of contesting her sister's greediness, Brit surrendered, "I had to let her bad behavior go," Brit said. "My mother gave me some beautiful pieces before she died. Those mean more to me now."   Because Brit's older sister had been so focused on getting her share of the loot, she had tromped on not only the boundaries of her younger sister, but also the wishes of her deceased mother. Brit Named that her sister had very toxic energy, and after the two siblings met to sprinkle their mother's ashes into the sea, Brit Claimed her energetic boundaries by deciding to respectfully back away from the alliance. The Reframe: Brit and her sister did not share the same values, and walking away from their relationship served the new frequency that Brit had chosen for herself and her family.

Zoe, a fifty-something, semi-retired nurse, called in need of an "emergency" coaching session. Her brother, in the midst of a very bitter divorce, had contacted her with a rather strange request: He wanted to use Zoe's name temporarily as a placeholder on piece of property he was purchasing. Her brother hoped to keep the purchase under the radar until he and his ex-wife had completed their court battles.

"When he first asked me for this favor my gut screamed 'HELL NO!" Zoe explained, "But we're a tight bunch and my heart intercepted my head which really wants to help him land securely in his new life."

Still wary of the deal, Zoe had asked the right questions. Her brother explained that he only needed to keep the purchase a secret until he and his ex-wife were out of probate.

"He told me it would cost me nothing and I would only hold title legally for three months, tops. Then we will transfer the title back to his name. No capital gains, so no tax implications."

As Zoe and I set to Name, Claim, and Reframe her dilemma with her brother, she revealed, "He and I are eighteen months apart and I can't remember my life without him. He is witty and has a big personality, yet when we are together, we trigger each other like we're little kids again. But, the truth is that I love him and would honestly offer him my kidney if he needed it. I trust that he would do the same for me. It is our pact, a never negotiated, unsigned, unspoken treaty. We don't hang out much, but when he calls, I pick up."

Zoe Named her feelings—Family loyalty and a sister's desire to soothe the pain of someone she loved. She had justified that her Claim (agreeing to help her brother) was the ultimate Gentle Warrior, above the line action, serving as her brother's bridge from point A to point B. "I told him, I'd get back to him tomorrow, but now I am not sure," she wavered.

Here's where the deal began to get slippery for Zoe and why she had asked for a thought partner. Zoe had not taken the time to Reframe how the action aligned with the integrity of her value boundaries. In her quest to serve her brother's needs, Zoe had convinced herself that her Claim matched her core values around family loyalty, but as we dove deeper into Zoe's dilemma, red flags began to trigger her underlying emotions. The first warning sign was that she had avoided telling her husband about the agreement. How could Zoe claim love, let alone loyalty, if she was afraid to tell her husband?

"Each time I look at my husband, I feel horrible, it all seems disloyal, like I am withholding an ugly secret . . . UGH!" she admitted. "This must mean I am well below and in the red zone of wounded responses!"

Withholding the agreement from her husband conflicted with the integrity of her values around family love and loyalty. Zoe's mind was also stuffed with all the unsavory ways that her brother's deal might undermine her own finances. Bottom line, the transaction felt like an ugly betrayal of trust that she could not risk introducing into her marriage. Our conversation helped her to bravely Name her fears and Claim an alternate action that better matched the truth inside the core of her essential self. Zoe's Reframe came in the form of an honest conversation with her brother about why she was saying "no." Although her decision to pass on the deal was resolute, her desire to connect with her brother was genuine and she worried that he would be angry.

"He was fine with it," she explained weeks later. "I am so glad I took time to dive back into my Name and Claim because in the interim my brother found an alternate solution that will serve his goals and keep me out of his mess."

If you feel moral conflict of any kind while negotiating a Reframe, stop, and go back to the Name and Claim steps, because something is definitely rubbing up against your core values. Part of guarding your boundaries is the freedom to reflect and then change your mind, which is exactly what Zoe decided to do.

While it is always tempting, it is not our place to tell our adult siblings what to believe or how to act. If we ever hope for connection, we must lean into compassion and accept that our adult sisters and brothers are doing the best they can.

In the end, you have got to live within your own truths. While Brit and Zoe's stories differ, in the end each sibling used their Reframe to shift their mindset so they could stand firmly in an action that aligned more with their essential self. Moral of the story: If you are ever in doubt at the Reframe stage, circle back around to Name and Claim. If you're really stuck, pulling the "Not my circus, not my monkeys" card is always the safest option.

Adult Children

Reframing as our children grow up and into adulthood is a whole different lane. I am a reformed helicopter parent who practices enormous restraint and self-management not to call, suggest, or offer opinions to either of my adult children (unless asked, of course). When either of them requires counsel, we can surmise what advice they are seeking by the parent they enlist for help. My husband, Bill, receives all the financial and career queries while I receive more of the interpersonal, etiquette and travel plan inquiries. Just like when they were growing up, our daughter tends to share more about her life than our son. This is most likely due to my past helicopter-parenting ways.

You are going to screw up eventually with your adult kids, get used to it! Your adult offspring are most likely averse to outside opinions, especially your unsolicited ones. You are not in control anymore and must hold your tongue or risk shame and temporary banishment. Just like when they were babies, you have no road map to navigate the twists and turns of the path and you have no idea what obstacles you might encounter along the way. It's like one of those carnival games where the targets move up and down and you can't get a clear shot. You can only focus on your inner work and learn new rules while trying to break old habits. Although you have risen to a new level of self-awareness, there are times when you must lean into humility and plea for forgiveness from your now adult children!

I credit our son Patrick with teaching me that boundaries and their borders are moving targets and must be managed carefully. Although my husband and I have become fluent in deciphering Patrick's verbal and non-verbal signals when we have violated one of his boundaries, Patrick's core beliefs have altered with age and hence, so have the edges of his value boundaries. Just like any person, his values are nuanced and have shape shifted as he has matured. The constant evolution of values enforces the fact that we cannot settle into any assumptions as the things that used to trigger us and/or him have changed. What was once off-limits as dinner table conversation is now perfectly acceptable, yet a benign mention of something else might set off a minefield of misunderstanding.

When your children leave the nest, your traditional parenting role is complete. It's time to stand back and give your adult children the space to navigate their own self-sovereignty. When they return, whether it is for holidays or to move back in during a pandemic, a recalibration of both parties' value systems needs to occur. Changes have happened for them and for you. You may have learned one way to Name, Claim and Reframe as a parent, but now there is a whole other level of engagement, expectations, and subsequent boundary violations to navigate!

When Patrick called to announce that he and his then girlfriend would be coming west to visit for a month in December during the pandemic. Bill and I were elated.

"We'll both be working remotely, Mom, so I think it best for us to rent an Air B&B," Patrick mused. "This way we can all have space to work during the day and then we can gather for dinners and such."

His idea was brilliant. We had learned the hard way that too many DeWitts working under one roof was a recipe for disaster, taxing not only to the strength of our internet, but our magnanimity toward each other. I immediately began searching for in-law rentals close to our home and found perfection three blocks away in a spacious over-the-garage conversion, complete with washer and dryer. I contacted the owner to tentatively reserve the space and then enthusiastically called Patrick with the news.

"It's expensive, honey, but Dad and I can help you financially," I offered.

An inhibited silence permeated the phone connection, and I heard my son breathe deeply and say in a polite tone.

"So generous of you, Mom, but we haven't even bought our plane tickets yet and it's too soon for us to commit. I will have to say no thank you for now."

It seems our 29-year-old son was better at Naming and Claiming than I was. He had successfully Named his frustration (his overzealous mother) and then Claimed a graceful boundary check that allowed him to stand firmly in the adult life he had created for himself in New York City.

I got the hint and Reframed our whole exchange immediately. "Oh, my goodness!" I thought to myself, a decade ago this exchange would not have been so cordial. In fact, Patrick may have even hung up on me.

With so many past mistakes and parental boundary violations under my belt, I recovered with the mindful Reframe of a Gentle Warrior: "Yikes... I'm sorry, Patrick, I am doing it again, trying to control your life. I'm so sorry for the misstep, please forgive me. Let me start again. When you are ready, please let us know how we can support your trip out west. We are so excited that you are coming!"

I had caught myself, in the act of helicopter-parenting and had promptly apologized. My Gentle Warrior was now influencing my thinking. Thankfully, Patrick was also accustomed to my old ways and received my confession with grace, kindness, and amusement. He and I are learning these new dance steps together. "Honey," I confessed, "can you tell that I am trying to self-manage my urges to NOT control everything? It is a daily practice, but today I caught myself. I promise I will continue to strengthen this new muscle. I love you." Patrick laughed, "I can tell you're trying, Mom, I love you too."

As we hung up the phone, I smiled to myself, knowing that part of becoming a Gentle Warrior is humility. Be kind to yourself, when we learn new practices, we're bound to have relapses and false starts. Always ask for forgiveness or at the very least, a second chance, especially with those you love.

The love interests that your children bring home will suddenly be intermingling with your house rules or value boundaries. Since your adult child clearly likes this person enough to bring them home, you are hoping for a well-behaved guest, at the very least.

Diane came to her coaching session for a Name, Claim and Reframe collaboration after a triggering visit from her college aged son, Ben, and his newly minted girlfriend during their spring break. Right out of the gate, Diane Named that her below the line mommy radar was triggered almost immediately by the young women's decorum.

"She was not only domineering towards our son, answering questions I directed to him, but she also had poor grammar," Diane admitted. "I know it's judgmental, but her 'Where's the butter at?' and 'No, I don't want none, thank you' really got under my skin."

Although the young woman had been friendly, as the evening rolled around, Diane noted that she did not hold her liquor well and grew boisterous and argumentative at the family dinner table. Instead of matching this lower frequency, Diane quietly took the wine back into the kitchen. Diane and her husband used discretion for the rest of their visit, having faith that their polite boundary would create the detachment they needed to honor their son's choice. Just before the Uber arrived to take the couple back to the airport, Ben hugged Diane and said earnestly, "Thank you for letting Rachel visit, Mom."

"I do not have a good poker face and our son knew that we were not impressed.", Diane laughed, "I hugged Ben tighter, and whispered into his ear, 'Of course, sweetheart, Dad and I love YOU-so much.' "

Diane had Claimed a higher frequency by creating a quiet boundary between the fierce love she had for her son and the way his girlfriend's below the line behavior had triggered her.

"She projects an enormous amount of below the line masculine energy," Diane shared. "What I can't be with is her verbally domineering behavior. Although we pray it will be a short romance, he seems to really like her."

"Okay, Diane, you've done an incredible job Naming what you can't be and Claiming a higher frequency," I confirmed for her. "What do you need to do to Reframe your mindset?"

"I think we need to ride it out and let the relationship run its course. Ben is away at college, so we aren't exposed to her very much. I have faith that he will see the light. I have to detach, or I might say something that will cause him to cling to her tighter," Diane answered.

I was proud of her work within herself as a Gentle Warrior with this situation.

Although Diane's Reframe created a boundary for her and her husband, it didn't last long. As the spring semester progressed, Ben called in the wee hours of the morning, distraught, as his girlfriend had verbally abused him publicly in a drunken haze. "She yelled, screaming that I would be unfaithful to her when I am home this summer." He was crying now, "Mom, she screamed, 'You'll ****" anything, I don't trust you!' " Diane, hearing the anguish in her 20-year old's voice, received him with compassionate love and nurturing acceptance.

"I chose to use prompts that addressed her behavior, not her as a person: 'What does it feel like to be in a relationship with someone who belittles you in public?' or 'What is missing from your relationship if she accuses you of cheating before you have left for the summer?' I sense that Ben already knew the romance was doomed but he needed us to help him sort it," she said confidently.

In detaching herself from her son's "choice," Diane Reframed her mindset by taking the role of trusted advisor, not protector.

In our next session, she reflected aloud: "It was not my job to tell or convince my son that he needed to break it off, instead it was my role to support Ben by listening and asking questions that might point him towards the values and boundaries he needed to Name and Claim."

Diane had supported her son, not by telling him her opinion but by listening to him with an attuned compassion. She got curious and had faith that her prompts would be the grounding cord to help her son choose his own path to safely.

"You already know what you need to do honey" she had told him on the phone.

Weeks later, during our session, Diane gave me an update. "He broke it off with her, thank goodness. Ben will be back home in a week to begin a summer internship. Hurrah!"

We have all been in dysfunctional relationships, and perhaps your children will too. Trust that they will shift and sort it out. If they ask for your counsel, take your ego out of it, step into your highest frequency by asking powerful questions that will help them to Name, Claim and Reframe the best course of action. On the other hand, if they marry someone, you are less than thrilled with, Name, Claim and then move to the Reframe step quickly!

By embracing the journey of the Name, Claim and Reframe process with family, we find the gift we were meant to receive. Even when you hit a dead end, the detour always has a purpose. Maybe you needed to slow down or were headed in the wrong direction and the roadblock gave you an opportunity to find a more authentic and heart-centered solution. Running marathons taught me much about how to live my life, one mile at time. When we fight the process by forcing it or over-training, we become injured. When I allowed myself time to fully heal from injury, I always came back stronger, more enlightened, and with a clearer vision. Time away to reflect always provides us opportunities to discover new perspectives and plan a new route through life's little entanglements. When we face up to those that we love using the virtues of our new frequency, we allow ourselves an incredible arsenal of tools and resourcefulness so we can take clear and consistent action to serve the ones who need us most.

Although my loyal heart is bursting with love for all those in my familial brood, I know now that it works best when I stay within the borders of my own power and authority. It's a delicate balance that includes self-care and a blind trust that everyone, including me, is doing the best that they can.

CHAPTER EIGHT

Name, Claim & Reframe

CRISIS

TIMES OF CRISIS WILL COME INTO YOUR LIFE WHERE YOU could not possibly imagine taking the time to reflect on the Name, Claim or Reframe process. You are in high stress survival mode, yet these times of crisis are when we must lean evermore into our essential selves. For people who might not be strong spiritually, faith can be a struggle. The beauty of Name, Claim and Reframe is that you don't need faith in any person but yourself. Alignment with our essential truths allows us to find the path up and out of the tenuous circumstances that have suddenly become our unexpected reality.

While greatness can often be found on the other side of catastrophe, a structure of support in the heat of the chaos ensures that we do not bend our core values or trigger an old wound that tips off a more unsavory below the line behavior pattern. Naming the emotions that we are experiencing in the crisis helps us to ground in courage and Claim the actions that will aid in survival while we wait for the Reframe.

While everyone's perceived standard of crisis may vary, how we support ourselves and those we love depends greatly on the tools we use to find our footing. Think back to the first time you got a flat tire. You are on the freeway, late for work and have no idea how to locate the spare or how to go about changing it. As the cars whiz past, you are in a reactive panic and dipping below the line: "No one cares about me, I am alone, I will be here all day."

Your phone has no charge, and you haven't sprung for a AAA membership. This is a crisis because you are stuck, with no way to call for assistance and no idea when help will arrive. After Naming your fear and victimhood, the universe intervenes. Help arrives in the form of a CHP officer who kindly helps you Claim an action by putting on the spare and directing you towards the nearest tire shop so they can remedy your situation. The crisis is averted, and you have Reframed your thinking for the next time you get a flat tire. It's not a crisis because you know what to do, where to go for help, and how navigate to safety. While the criteria for what qualifies as a disaster may vary greatly between ages and stages, crises are part of life, and everybody must face them in some way, shape, or form. Facing a crisis forces us to fall back on the truth within our essential self. We must Name the pain we feel and then take responsibility for it by Claiming an action that will ultimately help us Reframe the way we see the impact of the crisis. We emerge from these challenges changed because we have come face to face with our greatest fears and in doing so, discovered our deepest potential.

No one plans to parent a child through addiction, but when her family's crisis spiraled out of control, Cleo was desperate for a Reframe that she could integrate into a daily mindset. Her teenage daughter, Kristi, was off the rails. By her junior year in high school, Kristi had totaled a car and spent two nights in juvenile hall. Stuck in an endless loop, Cleo and her husband Jack were well versed in how to Name their emotions in the scenario and Claim above the line actions. They loved their daughter and would go to any lengths to help her—but they were trapped in trying to control an outcome that a parent just cannot control. Addicts need to want to get better before they can ultimately save themselves. Just as Cleo and Jack extinguished one fire, another would ignite. They had spent thousands of dollars to help Kristi overcome her demons (wilderness camp, family therapy, and a costly local rehabilitation center), but nothing had worked. Kristi continued to relapse, straining both family harmony and Cleo's once stable marriage.

Their situation was infused with shame as the community quietly ostracized their family and jungle drums boomed with gossip about their daughter, Kristi's, antics. The more Kristi acted out, and they felt the silent judgement of their community, the more they tried to make it go away by controlling outcomes.

Cleo, Jack, and Kristi existed in the agony of their Name and Claim loop for more than a year until the death of one of Kristi's closest friends, in a car crash, served as the catalyst to the girl's awakening. The tragic event was the turning point and moved the family to the Reframe step. In fact, it was Kristi who needed to take them over the hump. There was nothing the parents could do until Kristi was ready. Seeing her own mortality, a devastated Kristi begged her parents to send her back to rehab for one more try. Cleo's humility and her courage to stand in the truth about her daughter's addiction is what ultimately saved the family: "When we sent Kristi back to Wilderness Camp the second time, everyone judged us," Cleo offered. "We had already invested in many burning barns, but we leaned into faith, hope and love, and got really lucky."

Cleo was over the shame of other people's opinions and her daily practice of Name and Claim had gifted her the Reframe clarity to let outside judgments blow away with the wind.

"Recovery is not for people who need it,
it's for people who want it."

—ANONYMOUS

Cleo and Jack's courageous decision to invest again, by giving their daughter another chance, was more importantly grounded in an absolute faith that Kristi herself had Reframed the mindset she needed in order to take responsibility for her own recovery. With Kristi's readiness to do the hard work, Cleo and Jack's Reframe was the faithful surrender of turning the controls over to their daughter.

Kristi emerged from her second rehab experience transformed and full of gratitude to her family, the wilderness program that had saved her, and the new possibilities she now saw in front of her. She entered university on schedule with an enthusiastic interest in studying drug and alcohol counseling so she could help teens like herself. Kristi had come full circle, and even spent a summer interning at the wilderness camp that had help her get healthy again. Cleo's story brought to light that, for some, the process of Name, Claim and Reframe can sometimes take years to complete, especially when we are dealing with a chronic disease like addiction.

Yet illness comes in all forms and a health crisis can disrupt all aspects of your life, whether it's a chronic or life-threatening illness, such as cancer, or a major health event such as a stroke, heart attack, or a debilitating injury. Often these conditions develop unexpectedly, upsetting your life and causing chaos and uncertainty to wreak havoc on your mindset. You feel overwhelmed by waves of difficult emotions, fear, worry, anger, despair, or grief. Maybe you become numb, frozen by shock or the feeling that you will never be able to cope. The emotional upheaval can make it difficult to think straight and can lead to anxiety and depression.

Whatever your emotional response is to the situation, it's important to know that you can take back your power in the structure of Name, Claim and Reframe. Each part of the process provides opportunities to receive yourself with compassion, upgrade your energy frequency, and realign your perspective so you can ease mental anguish and navigate challenges with more optimism and strategic thinking. When we are grounded in the clarity of what is most important, we gain access to our own attuned resourcefulness.

Maura, an otherwise healthy forty-something client, discovered she that had a large benign tumor behind her ear canal. The slow growing mass had compromised her ability to hear in her left her, while another unrelated issue had caused significant hearing loss in her right ear. As she and I spoke on the phone, her much hated hearing aids enhancing the sound, Maura faced the reality of her dismal situation with cautious pragmatism:

"It's not cancerous so I could wait, but I want that sucker out, so I am having it removed as soon as possible. I refuse to be a victim to anything growing in my skull that I can't control." She then laughed and added, "And the good news is that it's not in my brain, so that's a blessing."

"How can I help you to create a structure of support as you approach your surgery date and prepare for the recovery that will follow?" I prompted.

"My family is terrified, and I want to stand in a solid plan so I can confidently proceed forward with conviction,"

"Let's pack your bags, metaphorically speaking, for this unplanned detour, Maura. What are the essential ingredients that you will need before, during and after your surgery?"

Together, Maura and I created a plan that included everything from the masculine/feminine traits she was wanted to embody, to the essential items, resources, and forms of support that she would require when she returned home from the hospital. She leaned into the concept of receiving help from all those who loved her. To soothe her family's anxiety, Maura enlisted the help of her husband, her teen-age children, and her sacred circle, which include me as her coach. Maura made lists of what she needed to pack for her hospital stay, asked her sister to organize a meal train and recruited her son to coordinate post-surgery email updates to those lucky enough to be part of her inner sanctum. By the time Maura's surgery date arrived, she was grounded in her core value around optimism, and was confident that her receptive mindset would support her courageous decision to have the benign mass extracted.

The nine-hour surgery was a success, but when Maura came home, she realized immediately that, even with all her careful planning, the speed of her recovery was out of her control and Reframing this unfortunate plot twist would take longer than expected. The surgery, which had involved cutting into her skull to remove the lemon sized mass, had left painful incisions behind her ear that were very sore and swollen. Bright lights bothered her eyes and she suffered from fatigue as she managed nausea, sleepless nights, and the pain of recovery.

Although Maura and I texted back and forth during her first few weeks of recovery, we didn't speak on the phone until two months after her surgery.

"It was a lot more difficult than I anticipated," she admitted. "The first few weeks were pure hell, Andrea," she confessed. "Kind of like having a horrible hangover. Noise and bright lights were the worst and I basically just laid in bed for 3 weeks."

"Besides the physical healing piece, what can I do to support your transition back to real life?" I asked.

"I am both frustrated and embarrassed by these horrid hearing aids. They make me look like an old hag," she complained. "If I am ever to leap back into my role at work, I am really going to find a way to change my attitude towards them."

"What if we could somehow shape-shift this perspective and instead transform your hearing aids into an essential part of the original plan that we created before your surgery?" I offered

"You mean like make them my helpful sidekicks?" she laughed.

"*Exactly,*" I said. "Now let's brainstorm some sidekick characters that you won't mind tagging along as you Reframe what life might look like in the future."

Maura loved this idea and soon stole Shrek's Sidekick, Eddie Murphy's smart-ass Donkey, as the "large eared" identity for her hearing aids. She even named the left one, Eeyore and the right Eleanor. When we spoke next, she introduced me to each of them, sharing their quirky personality traits.

Two weeks later she reported great results post-surgery.

"After my hearing test, I show a 50% improvement in my hearing in the Eeyore ear. The doctor says I should expect this to increase to maybe even 75% in time. Eleanor in the right ear is not quite as promising, but she is trying her best."

I was thrilled that this playful and fun solution had not only worked, but Maura had discovered that integrating them into her recovery gave her sovereignty to embrace and accept where she had found herself in life at the moment.

"My donkeys are the best, Andrea. I've got them hooked up straight to my I-Phone and I can hear you loud and clear." She laughed. "And I can even 'hitch' those two little burros up to my computer for Zoom calls. I am back in the saddle again," she whooped.

"Now *there's* a healthy Reframe, Maura," I cheered "You are one tough dame!" Although her recovery from the surgery was a slow but steady process, Maura curated a mindset that helped her to heal from the inside out. Six months after our conversation, she flew to Boston to for her daughter's college graduation, Eeyore in her left ear and Eleanor in her right.

"Life is tough darling, but so are you."

—STEPHANIE BENNETT-HENRY

Divorce is a crisis that affects almost half of the American population. It is never an easy scenario to navigate, especially when money and kids are involved. I have watched desperate women grasp at their fallen egos, expecting that the husband that just left them will change his mind and suddenly rescue them from their peril. I have also watched women look at this life crisis as a wakeup call, urging them forward to meet their highest self. The uncoupling of any long-term relationship feels like a crisis but the conflicted emotions that accompany its demise can be Named, and a new viewpoint Claimed. Those who are being left behind often lead with the below the line energies of anger and victimhood. They have mistakenly given the controls to someone else, surrendering their fast-sinking ship to yesterday's dreams, not today's truths and opportunities.

Beth was blindsided when her husband, Bob, hired a courier to serve her with divorce papers at her front door. To top it off, Bob had cowardly planned a business trip so that he would be on a plane and unavailable to answer her outraged call. Distraught, Beth called her closest friend for support and soon found her reality splashed across the neighborhood phone lines, the shock and shame of it all blistering the fresh wounds within her heart.

Devastated, Beth, came to coaching to Name and Claim her unforeseen circumstance, and boldly Reframe a new future for herself and her three teenage daughters. After sitting with the anger and hurt brought on by the divorce, Beth began to settle into the terror of job hunting.

"What can I do to model independence for my teenage daughters?" she asked me.

"Curiosity is the antidote to fear, Beth. What are you curious to learn? What is something you've always wanted to do, but never had the courage try?" I inquired.

Beth was silent for a moment and then spoke with great clarity. "I've always wanted to study to become a real estate broker. I love watching the market, pursuing open houses, and imagining all the ways to improve their curb appeal."

Beth's desire to step into the fire for her girls conjured the courage she needed to make a plan so she could stake a very solid Claim in herself—earning a real estate license, joining a local, upscale company and selling homes in the very community that had shamed her embarrassing circumstance six months earlier.

Beth had discovered the fortitude of herself within this unforeseen storm. As the dust settled, Beth Reframed a new life for herself that better matched who she had become at the height of the siege, a fiercely brave working woman who had learned to live on a budget.

"I decided that I needed to take control," she said. "As angry as I was from the shame of how our marriage ended, I got busy building my life raft. I did not want to be Bob's victim anymore, so I made a plan that would serve me and my girls."

Beth had more reframing to do and when her youngest daughter graduated from high school, she sold her house and bought a beautifully updated townhouse that better suited that her empty nest lifestyle. Beth not only survived the crisis, she had thrived in the face of it and stood resolutely as the independent woman she had hoped to Claim at the very beginning of her crisis.

"Start over, my darling. Be brave enough to find the life
you want and courageous enough to chase it. Then start
over and love yourself the way you were always meant to."

—MADALYN BECK

If we are honest with ourselves, nothing in life is sacred. One moment
you are enjoying a family vacation in Hawaii and then the next, you are
in search of a job and wondering if you can afford to buy your daughter's
track shoes. Having a crisis in your life demands an immediate trim-
ming of anything extraneous. When you intentionally focus on having
autonomy, you allow yourself to recalibrate a life that will serve you and
those you love. As scary as it can be, we always have the power to take
the wheel and proactively choose again.

It is through the Name and Claim process that we gain clarity on
what is most important so we can create a blueprint for an action that
will allow us to Reframe, heal and move on. Other people's opinions
keep us trapped in the old way of thinking, depleting our resources when
we should be focused on finding the hidden insight, opportunity, or frequency upgrade within the crisis. Reframing breaks the old, stale patterns
of the past so that we can expand our views with new perspectives which
will lead us into the future.

Navigating a crisis is an opportunity to cut through the illusion of
what was, so we can boldly choose again what will be. Never underestimate the power of trusting in yourself and the magnificence that lives
within your core. Life is all about how you recover, and sometimes your
back up plan turns out to be more sparkly than the disillusioned Plan A
you once clenched so tightly.

CHAPTER NINE

Name, Claim & Reframe

THE REAL WORLD

After practicing Name, Claim and Reframe with our family and the people inside of our sacred circle, integration of these practices out in the real world requires a sharper scrutiny and an earnest exploration. We are more readily triggered, must process feedback from well-meaning mentors and friends, and discover how the shapeshifting of our value boundaries affects our real-world perceptions.

As we discussed in Chapter Six, although everyone has an opinion, every opinion isn't necessarily a good match for where you are headed. There will also be energetic boundary violations, toxic energy to avoid, and plenty of monkeys and circuses that are not yours to tame. You are becoming more skilled at Reframing your mindset with each situation that you encounter. Celebrate that you are making progress, breaking old patterns, and fine tuning the skills necessary to live as a Gentle Warrior. I can assure you that as you busy yourself recalibrating how you are showing up in the world, you will experience healthier and more prosperous outcomes.

Here's the tricky part: because you have done the hard work to gain clarity about where you stand and what is most important, you may become triggered by unexpected sources, viewpoints and institutions that no longer match up with your new frequency. It's happened to all of us, we learn that someone we greatly admire and have placed on a pedestal is just another imperfect human being. Whether it happens through a triggering interpersonal exchange or an action that we witness, we become disillusioned that our great teacher has their own blind spots and flaws. When taken off guard, in the heat of the moment, we freeze, retreat, and make ourselves smaller so we can salvage the uncomfortable emotions we are experiencing.

You have the opportunity here to Name your disillusionment and the feelings that accompany it, and then lean into the Claim of the moment so you can recalibrate your grand expectations. Tanya Geisler warns against what she calls the "canonization" of leaders, celebrities, or anyone whose work we admire.

> "It CAN be a complicated relationship: we see someone doing something we admire, then project a kind of glory onto them (which is an illusion, to be sure), then start to compare ourselves to that shine, then feel "less so," then feel ugh, and then we have nowhere to go but to try to cut them down . . . especially when their human flaws start to show up . . . Who wants THAT? Who wants to be placed on a pedestal only to get shoved off?"
>
> —TANYA GEISLER, *Your Impeccable Impact*

The truth is that when we have these revelations of humanity, they are hinged on an opportunity for us to stand in our values and power, and accept that our guides and leaders are human, navigating their own core wounds, triggers, and false identities. We have been given the opportunity to redefine the power that we bestow on others while forging new paths of learning for ourselves.

Retaliation in the moment is a below the line reaction and while I wouldn't say that it can't be effective in certain contexts, I think when we reflect on the scenario and take a beat to explore our authentic feelings, we are often able to cultivate a response that aligns more closely with the integrity of our truths. As you understand your core values and how you choose to be treated and seen, you can explore different responses that reflect this upgraded frequency. How will you know where you stand if you do not begin to practice drawing that line in the sand?

The birthing of Name, Claim and Reframe became an essential tool and the brainchild for this book as I struggled to find a way to resolve an embarrassing exchange with a thought leader I will call X. This incident happened at one of her leadership workshops. Although I had followed her on Instagram, listened to her podcast and used her curriculum with clients for months, as a newly minted coach, I was excited to mingle with other like-minded women and take a deeper dive into X's thought leadership. My colleagues, an eclectic assortment of women leaders from all over the Bay Area, gathered for a day-long workshop to explore rich teachings that wove the tenants of feminine leadership with practical tools we could adapt and utilize in our varied professional roles. Towards the end of the day, I bravely raised my hand to ask a question. As I stood up to address, X, a woman I greatly respected, my heart raced, and I called up my confident essential self to present my query to the community.

"There are times when I use this tool and I feel very 'lame' because..."
X stopped me mid-sentence.

"HOLD ON, stop for a moment. Is anyone offended by the word that Andrea just used? The use of the word, 'lame' could be misinterpreted, and we certainly don't want to make anyone feel excluded or uncomfortable," she warned.

The confidence I had called in seconds earlier, quickly retreated and was immediately replaced by my shadow-version of self-doubt. It felt like X had just "shamed" me publicly, hanging me out on a limb, alone and unsupported. The word "lame" had clearly triggered her: a fear of political correctness prompted by a vernacular term that conjured her shadow-version of self to show up. I realized immediately that my definition of "lame", which I used to describe my own imperfection, had been misinterpreted as an offensive term meant to taunt or ridicule someone who was crippled. To save herself from appearing to condone my *political incorrectness*, X, had thrown me under the bus, thus humiliating me publicly. A skilled facilitator, she recovered with grace. I did not, and the burr under my skin began to fester.

In the moment, having not yet developed the structure of Name, Claim and Reframe, I acquiesced to her below the line redirect. "My sincere apologies, please let me rephrase the question," I repented.

I waited for someone in the room to step forward with an objection against my poor word choice, but none were submitted. My face turned crimson as everyone in the ballroom had just witnessed my cultural incompetence and insensitivity. X smiled warmly and said, "Thank you, Andrea."

I chose in that moment not to call out her obvious misinterpretation of my word choice or the public shaming she had bestowed upon me. Despite how badly I felt about my awkward phraseology, I was mortified and felt very misunderstood. Remember, I am standing up in ballroom for all to see. I recovered by reacting, I apologized and then swiftly searched for a synonym to repair my now obvious blunder.

I inserted the word "inept" and proceeded with my question. The paraphrase aptly described not only the feeling I had about the tool we that were discussing, but myself at that moment. When we find ourselves in a situation like this, we must first Name it: What about this (situation) has your undies in a bunch?

That evening, as I drove home from the workshop, I Named the trigger, her passive aggressive interjection seemed power grabbing. X, who I had placed high on a pedestal of admiration, had not modeled thoughtful feminine leadership for me, in that particular moment. Instead of being proactive and engaging me in a dialogue about my word choice so she could gain further clarification, she had been reactive to first save her own image.

My embarrassment soon turned to anger and I Claimed an action that remedied my outrage with what I now realize was an above the line response. I could not go on unless I communicated, in a graceful, sophisticated, Gentle Warrior way, that I had felt disrespected. I would not accept being dismissed carelessly, especially in a public forum. My outrage was further fueled by the fact that her workshop was expensive, and she had delivered the reprimand within the tenants of her own feminine-infused leadership curriculum. While I understood how my poor word choice had been triggering, her actions oozed with hypocrisy. I needed to Claim my integrity by advocating for myself. The day after the workshop, I made the bold decision to email X with a request to discuss the incident.

As I Named the emotions I was experiencing, the ambidextrous flavor of the situation had hooked my inner critic into a loop of self-doubt, so I sought the additional support of my mentor coach at the time, Abigail, who concurred that the use of the word "lame" on my part was not a capital offense. Abigail further supported me by asking, "Do you want to be right, Andrea, or do you want to learn?" I had put my foot squarely into it and now I wanted to grow, Claim a new boundary, and most importantly, Reframe the situation so I could expand and grow into the power I knew that I possessed as a leader.

If we can target what we are bothered by, it becomes easier to strategize how to reconcile. In my case, I chose to reach out to X. In the correspondence, I apologized again for my poor word choice and went on to explain how the interaction had landed on me. While I waited for her response, I tried to remove my ego with a sincere reflection to better understand the situation from X's point of view. What about my actions triggered X's reaction? Most likely it had nothing to do with me and everything to do with her concerns about political correctness and her public image as a thought leader.

When we step away and take a meta-view of the situation, it is easier to empathize with the actions or reactions of others. It's usually not personal and has more to do with them than it does with us. There must be certitude when we stand up for ourselves and complete our own personal work, especially when we feel we have not been seen, heard, or respected. I concluded that I had been caught in a situation where I had been unjustly accused of cultural incompetence. But truthfully, the incident made me question my outspoken presence, core persona and candor. I had unfinished learning to complete if I was to move on to the Reframe step, so I got curious. I wanted to understand more about the challenges that thought leaders face, especially when facilitating in a live setting. How did X navigate hiccups like mine, not only in her workshop offerings, but when serving on a panel or in a corporate setting? How did she consistently manage poise and grace, even while in the hot seat? The reflection also helped me gain awareness of the generational differences that often exist in American language. Just as my use of a vernacular term had offended someone fifteen years my junior, I had seen and heard slang terms that I did not understand, and some that I found offensive. I made efforts to embrace my own imperfection, while also committing to ask for clarity when I encountered ambiguous linguistic terms in the future.

By the time I had processed the whole incident, I heard back from X, who kindly invited me to talk by phone so we could discuss things further. Although I was genuinely nervous about our meeting, hearing her sincere voice on the other end of the line, gave me peace of mind that we were meeting somewhere in the middle: two colleagues, each contrite in her own actions. I used the opportunity, not to stand in my outrage but to pick her brain so I could learn. I came away feeling seen, heard, and vindicated. She was generous, poised, and professional, modeling for me how seasoned and practiced leaders navigate adversity. It was a constructive and informative discussion and I appreciated and enjoyed our conversation. While I walked away from our dialogue with new insights and gratitude for her expanded perspectives, my admiration for her had lost some of its luster. She had sacrificed someone else's dignity for her own. However, I had been quite successful in modeling for myself the compassionate thoughtful leadership of a Gentle Warrior.

The experience also changed the expectations that I had falsely created for X and for all thought leaders whose work I admire. It is unfair for us to place anyone we admire on a high and mighty pedestal of perfection. We as humans are multi-faceted and learn not through triumphs, but rather by Reframing our missteps.

"Humility is born of the spirit,
Humiliation of the ego."

—ALAN COHEN

The intimate conversation that we shared revealed that X also struggled to understand the blurred lines and unforeseen triggers of being in the public eye. She was polite, but also cautious with her remarks, which I sensed came from the public persona that she had created to protect her boundaries. X had been very generous to meet with me, but she did so to protect her reputation and her brand. As I took in her elegant diplomacy, I wondered what she might share if her guard was down, and she trusted me with her secrets and the things she may have learned the hard way. I'll never know, but I will always be grateful to her because she was clear on her core values which gave her the courage to lean into this potentially difficult conversation and helped her to stand firmly in the integrity of her brand. If we ignore our truth to avoid conflict and to keep the peace, we only start a war within ourselves.

The experience was significant because in the struggle to Name, Claim and Reframe the integrity of myself, I found the Gentle Warrior I had become. She Named what she couldn't be with, Claimed an above the line response and Reframed it by harvesting another woman's brilliant wisdom. While I gained closure, insight, and clarity by circling back after the fact, most of us don't have this luxury. In order to deepen my learning, I needed to get curious about how I might have addressed the issue right there, in the heat of the moment. Of course, with proper reflection, we can always think of the perfect response, yet my goal from this query was to Claim another theoretical portal that could be used should a similar situation arise in the future. Emotions can hinder our ability to stand in our power, but, what if instead of becoming submissive, we are triggered to go below the line masculine and become territorial or confrontational? This is exactly what we hope to avoid as Gentle Warriors in the making. When we encounter conflict, we have two choices: we can run, or we can rise.

Let's open a scenario for you to practice Name, Claim and Reframe with someone who triggers or throws you off course from your expectations or idealization of this person. In a conversation, you realize suddenly that you have been misunderstood, falsely accused, or unjustly labeled as culturally incompetent.

NAME: You quickly Name your emotion (embarrassed, rejected, attacked) and then recalibrate it by catching yourself BEFORE you dip below the line.

CLAIM: You Claim an alternate response that embodies the upgraded energy you hope to personify. "Oops, what just happened? I've got my heart in my hand and it feels like I've been abandoned out on a limb. I feel very vulnerable, but I also sense that I have said something terribly wrong. Let's find a way to back track so I can understand how my language might have triggered you."

As you lean into your feelings of vulnerability and you take ownership of how your actions may have hurt someone else, you extend an olive branch that acknowledges fault on your end, yet also holds firm that a value boundary was crossed for you. By leaning into humility, you offer the other party an opportunity to collaborate, so together you can agree upon next steps. While an apology would most certainly be appropriate, the goal and hope here is that the other party might meet you halfway so you can work together to find a peaceful resolution. You must also be willing to accept with grace any regrets on their end. We must stand firm here, receiving any anger respectfully, and any differing opinions with poise and compassion.

REFRAME: By acknowledging how you felt in the heat of the moment, you have advocated for your value boundaries, while also taking bold ownership for actions that may have hurt another. There is much to learn here as we stand in our power in an above the line fashion. We expand our perspective because we are aware of generational variances in language, especially vernaculars. We practice honesty and humility which are helpful tools in negotiation.

You can use this structure anywhere, applying it to minor disputes with your partner, or contentious conflicts with a coworker. It can create more harmonious interactions, especially with those you hold most dear. When we take time to respond authentically in our truth, we dance in the way of a Gentle Warrior. Once we understand what values we are honoring, it becomes easier to curate actions that preserve the boundaries of our essential self. Since life is unknown much of the time, we can't predict what our inner or outer circle will throw our way. When we use practices that uphold the higher frequencies of who we have become, we stand firmly in self-sovereignty.

Even when we are triggered and overreact, an apology is an act of maturity that demonstrates a sincere desire to maintain harmony and understanding with others. Taking ownership by apologizing shows your strength of character. It is a sign of someone who is courageous, humble, and open-minded. If we are to boldly stand within the borders of our core beliefs, we must take responsibility for our part in any conflict. An apology is an act of kindness that shows respect. It is also an important step in conflict resolution. Apologies have healing power, whether you are apologizing to a client, your boss, a family member, a friend or a stranger. When we lead with our heart instead of an armored-up and ego-driven need to be right mindset, we walk in the way of the Gentle Warrior. Choose to be the person who initiates the apology and do it with a generous and authentic heart. You will grow to be the person others look up to and your organization, brand, or the DNA you represent will be better served in the end.

CHAPTER TEN

Managing Your Gentle Warrior

EVEN WHEN YOU HAVE NAMED, CLAIMED, AND REFRAMED, you are no messiah on the hill. Your internet will still go out, your husband will forget to pick up the dry cleaning, your six-year-old will use unsavory language that you taught them unintentionally, someone will steal your parking place, and you will find yourself on the freeway in the one lane that is not moving. You are dangerously close to a below the line reaction and are suddenly asking yourself, "Where am I and what do I need to do to take charge of this situation?" The universe will test you when it is time for you to elevate to a higher frequency, so honor how much work you have done and see that these events are an integral part of your evolution to walk in the way of a Gentle Warrior. It is about catching yourself and choosing to proceed with introspection and an attuned vision.

Mindfulness is useless if your balanced mindset evaporates once you get up off the sofa. When I am with my essential self, my Gentle Warrior, she may not know exactly what she is going to do, but she will choose a thoughtful, above the line, response. She receives me, meaning that I receive myself, with grace, compassion and understanding. I Name where I have found myself. I breath in, I breath out, and because I have done the introspective work to be a Gentle Warrior, I Claim an above the line action that will serve me much better in the long run. I will be grounded because I have skillfully caught the core wound and possibly even that false identity that previously triggered me. I Reframe that moment with intention having made the bold choice not be a reactive warrior any longer.

In order to do the daily work of a Gentle Warrior, we need to be clear on where we stand on an hourly basis. We separate from the armed parts of ourselves so we can lead with the attuned grace of our disarmed resourcefulness. I am not saying it is going to be easy, but you will experience more ease and flow in your life when you make the choice to Name, Claim and Reframe. That choice is a commitment. When you revert to the old habits of hiding, or breaking your boundaries, the garb will feel heavy and laden, like you are putting on a cloak of false self. There is no turning back once you have done the work. Your spirit is calling you towards an unburdened freedom that requires that you stand firmly in the truth of your essential self.

Breath and Meditation

It sounds counterintuitive after all the action steps I have given you, to take that stillness is the ultimate key to true Gentle Warrior-hood, but intuitive living starts by learning how to be still with yourself. The first way to become aligned your essential self, your Gentle Warrior, is to simply breathe. To notice that you need to stop spinning so you can mindfully choose your next step forward. This simple act not only takes awareness, but it also takes discipline, focus, and the versatility to create a pocket in time so you can make a plan. If you are going to start a big project, take a new life direction, or simply upgrade the frequency in which you live, you have to make the decision to commit to being mindful.

Intrigued by the healing power of meditation, I too wanted to experience the state of bliss it can bring. Determined and desperate to achieve mindfulness, I fought the act of stillness much like a warrior who runs from her pain. My fidgety monkey mind focused on everything but the breath that was supposed to escort me into the ease and flow of presence

When you first put yourself on a mindfulness schedule, it can feel like an arduous and frustrating obligation. When I committed to start a meditation ritual, I was ashamed of my inability to calm my bustling mind. I pretended to meditate and then used the time to make endless lists, focus on tasks left undone, and then berate myself for doing so. The more determined I got about achieving stillness, the harder it became. I made note of all the reasons why giving up made me a failure. The point of mindfulness is self-love and because I refused to be alone with myself, I only managed to achieve self-hate. When we drop into ourselves, there is no place to hide. We must receive ourselves and our emotions in the raw. Meditation without awareness around how to Name core wounds and false identities and Claim above the line energy is like trying to rope in a tornado. Without these steps, your funnel cloud of wayward thoughts will destroy any semblance of peace and harmony.

I struggled to meditate because I had not yet accepted the true source of my emotion and honestly feared who (or what) I might encounter inside the sanctuary of myself. I worried more about how I might manage all of the rage and the pain bottled-up inside, rather than the mindful state I might achieve if I confronted the torrent of storms hidden beneath my armor.

Author and Buddhist monk, Jack Kornfield, says that "Free is not free of feelings, but free to feel each one and let it move on, unafraid of the movement of life."

We must compassionately Name our fears and their entourage of demons so we can acknowledge all the parts of our wholeness, especially the untamed and messy bits. There are thousands of guided meditations available online, some only 2 or 3 minutes long. We all have the power to be our own gurus. Lean in and get curious about what mediation is like for you, not anyone else. If full-on meditation is as much of a struggle for you as it was for me, we will start with breathing. Breathing will do wonders by keeping your mind busy on that simple task so you can detach from what is and drop into what could be.

Breathing exercises are a great place to start because they require no special equipment. The best part is that they can be done anywhere. Start by gifting yourself just one deep grounding breath, this is all that is needed to initiate your exploration. When we are stressed, we hold our breath, allowing stagnate CO_2 to stifle our thinking. Breath is your portal to cast out the old and call in the three big O's: oxygen, opportunity, and optimism. You are making the choice to exhale below the line reactivity so you can replace it with an empowered above the line response. When you breathe out your angst, you make room for your Gentle Warrior to step forward and impact your thinking.

Breathing Exercises

Easy Breathing Practice: Get comfortable. This breathing technique will probably come more naturally than all of the other techniques. Similar to when your doctor asks you to breathe deeply during a chest exam, you'll find this technique engages your mind and breath fully.

- *Breathe* in through your nose until your belly fills with air
- *Breathe* out slowly through your nose
- Put one hand on your heart-space and the other on your belly and *breathe* in
- The hand on your stomach should rise more than the one on your chest
- *Breathe* out and feel your belly lower
- Repeat three more times

Simple Breath Focus: Focusing on your breath can help you push other anxious thoughts out of your mind. It allows you to concentrate solely on your breath and filling your lungs fully.

- Take a few deep breaths to get started
- Imagine you are breathing in calm and goodness
- When you breathe out, imagine you are exhaling your negativity and stress
- Continue for several minutes

Equal Breath Counts: As you practice this technique, you will be able to increase your inhale and exhale count. This exercise allows you to really focus on breathwork and keeping a "balance" within your diaphragm.

- Inhale and exhale for the same count
- Start with a slow count of five in
- Hold the breath for a count of five
- Exhale for your breath for slow count of five
- Repeat for several minutes

Through this simple breath focus, you begin a mini-meditation practice so you can experience the benefits of receiving yourself in whatever state of mind you are experiencing in that moment. Breathing is not only an effective grounding tool, but it slows the heartbeat, stabilizes blood pressure, and reduces anxiety. It won't happen all at once, but as you surrender with curiosity, you will learn to drop in with more trust and ease. After you feel like you are comfortable with the breathing, you can take another try at your "meditation practice." Meditation is imperfect and different each time you drop in, so cut yourself some slack and don't judge your mind's to-do lists. Just like that unsettled weather on the outside that has nothing to do with your inner world, acknowledge any rogue thoughts and then allow them to pass on through. The American Buddhist nun, Pema Chodron said, "You are the sky. Everything else is just weather." Should your mind start racing, go back to one of the breathing exercises. Take your time and know that this is the second level to Name, Claim and Reframe. You can feel confident that I have given you all the tools to execute this three-part system, and now you are learning how to do it moment by moment intuitively. Soon you will be receiving yourself like a trusted old friend who loves you unconditionally. By tenderly Naming your repressed emotion, you create a sanctuary to replenish your internal energy so that you can Claim an above the line action and Reframe the situation with a mindset that is more aligned with your core values and boundaries.

Some of my clients do not love the idea of meditation, so I suggest that they do "proactive meditation"—integrate a solitary activity into their daily routine that encourages introspection and detachment. The basic goal is to get them out of their heads and into their bodies so they are more open to the flow of a Name, Claim and Reframe recovery. The Japanese have perfected these little daily escapes into a practice called forest bathing or "*Shinrin-yoku*". *Shinrin* means "forest," and *yoku* means "bath." So *Shinrin-yoku* means bathing in the forest atmosphere or taking in the forest through our senses. This is not exercise, or hiking, or jogging, it is simply being in nature, connecting with it through our senses of sight, hearing, taste, smell, and touch. *Shinrin-yoku* is a form of meditation that opens our senses and bridges the gap between us and the natural world. I suggested the practice to Jess, a CPA who lives in an urban setting.

"I have been going out midday, during the week. I take in a bit of sunshine, receive the scents of whatever flora is blooming in the park and ask people if I can pet their dogs. Last week I packed a bag lunch and met a friend for a mini picnic. A thirty-minute forest bath does wonders, and I am avoiding those mid-afternoon slumps of my past, when I ate too many carbs."

When these clients go into nature, they return from their quiet moments lighter, more attuned with themselves, and ready to consistently practice Name, Claim and Reframe. If you keep at it, you will soon begin a courageous conversation with your true essence, your Gentle Warrior. It's about allowing ourselves to feel, think, and ground in a more heart-centered mindset. Think of the impact we could have if more of us took time to collect ourselves by using proactive meditation practices. The wise essence that lives under your armor is compassionate, gentle, and very brave, and she knows the way through. Once you start to connect with this part of yourself each day, you will find that you will strive to live only in this way. Of course, there are those days where we get thrown for a loop and need to stop, drop, and furiously roll ourselves into the structure of Name, Claim and Reframe. In a way, those days are what solidify and hone our skills as Gentle Warriors. It's the bloody battles that give us the best opportunities to find out what we are made of. When you Name your truth, you find your essential self.

I argue that anyone who does not believe in their inner resourcefulness has not yet dared explore the wellspring available within the sanctuary of self. They have not yet aligned with their Gentle Warrior.

Grounding

We all have the capacity to achieve a form of mindful presence. The rewards will most certainly change you for the better. The days that you fear looking inward are the days that stillness will benefit you the most. When you understand the truth within yourself, you awaken, and clarity shines a light on the path forward.

On the days that you can't get to formal meditation, make an intention to use moments like while you are in the shower, making breakfast, or watering the plants. Introspection allows you to hear your truths clearly: "How am I doing?" "What do I need?" "How can I celebrate myself today?"

Amidst the uncertainties of life, daily rituals and routines offer the opportunity to sink into the present moment and really savor it. While it may seem silly, the act of making your bed, feeding the cat, or wiping down the shower each morning provides your psyche with positive reinforcement through feeling productive. These simple tasks have a positive effect that carries over into the rest of the day and promotes a predictable flow that grounds us in purpose.

After Lesley moved to a new apartment, she struggled to develop a consistent morning routine. In this new setting, she felt detached from herself, which could lead to conflict and agitation later in the day. She wanted to ground herself by creating a morning ritual that would help her to connect with her essential self. Since she loved riding her bike to work, instead of riding the bus, she committed to cycling three days a week. It offered her legitimate exercise and she found that she arrived at the office more balanced and focused.

Heather, a working mother with two children under the age of four, felt harried, impatient, and resentful. An introvert who desperately needed to carve out time to collect herself, Heather gave herself two hours each weekday morning before her children woke up. She rose at 5:00am and made a sacred mug of strong coffee and enjoyed some uninterrupted quiet time. She sweetened the practice by not holding firm to any one activity. While some mornings she chose yoga, meditation or journaling, other mornings she met a friend for a brisk walk and coffee talk. "It is 'me-time' to do whatever I damn well please," Heather said triumphantly.

Even when sometimes it feels like all we are doing is treading water, when we practice self-sovereignty to achieve deeper understanding, we discover an untapped abundance of courage and resilience that has the potential to lead us to the upgraded frequency of ourselves.

Grounding could also be the simple act of getting out and experiencing other people's energy—the buzz of a sporting event or enjoying music in community with other human beings. Sitting in a restaurant or walking through a public space reminds us that we are part of something much greater than the little things that trigger and annoy us. I have made people-watching a pastime, other beings energize me as I mix my energy with those around me.

It doesn't matter what you do, find something that fills you so you can replenish yourself, move your energy around and elevate yourself to the higher frequency that is calling you. Make a habit of never putting the key to your own happiness in someone else's pocket. When we engage our minds daily in the intellectual inquisitiveness of introspection, it expands our awareness so we can shore up and salve the parts of us that need attention. The daily intention of checking in with myself softens my harder edges so I can show up in a more thoughtful, strategic, and realistic manner. Even when my temper flares, calling myself into a more grounded state slows me down so I can Name emotions and remedy the situation going forward. Wouldn't you rather be proactive than reactive?

If you feel unease, dare to explore yourself from the inside out. Curiosity is what separates happy people from unhappy people. Those who are at one with their truest essence have the perfect balance between who they are at the core, what they are feeling in the moment, and how they want to dance with the external world. As former first lady, Eleanor Roosevelt said wisely, "No one can make you feel inferior without your consent."

The key ingredients of a well lived life revolve around the things we value most— the need for connection with those we love, being disciplined around practicing self-sovereignty, extending kindness towards others, and having the resourcefulness to know when your inner reserves have been depleted. What do you need to feel balanced and whole and how will you ensure you maintain a Gentle Warrior mindset on a daily basis?

When I launch with a new client, the first part of our journey together is core value boundary exploration. There is a lucidity that emerges when we use our values to make life decisions, especially when the unexpected darkens our doorstep. Your child has a learning disability, you are laid off work, or you are diagnosed with a chronic disease. The Tsunami has derailed your life and you need a plan of action. You can react, fighting against the force of the wave, or you can build an architecture that will allow you to ride the current of the storm. Values are the foundation for a well lived life, especially when things go south.

A New Way of Living

Now that we have learned grounding into ourselves through pausing, breathing routines, and meditation, we can ready ourselves for the world at large. With all you have learned about triggers, core wounds, and the why behind your core beliefs, you have done the work to unravel and understand the evolution of yourself.

Use the set of tools that I have presented within the structure of Name, Claim and Reframe to support your evolution:

- Balance Your Response (page 24)
- How to Claim and Tame of Your Inner Critic (page 63)
- Core Value List (page 95)
- Core Value Mini Assessment (pages 97–98)
- Build-Your-Land Exercise (page 118)
- Reframing Feedback Exercise (page 132)
- Reframing Compliments (page 139)
- Gentle Warrior Toolbox (page 141)
- Breathing Exercises (page 185)

Use the prompts from the Gentle Warrior Toolbox and put them near your desk at work, by your bed or in your car so you can remember the shortcuts and quick routes out of sticky, challenging, or awkward situations. This practice is self-care in its purest form, making a habit of filling yourself first before you fill everyone else.

We will be challenged in our commitment to embody Gentle Warriors everywhere we go. Some days may be smooth sailing, while other days we will be blindsided by someone who is spiritually asleep, clueless, or downright mean. I am constantly recalibrating my mindset so I can catch myself before I dip below the line, my essential self-stepping up to ask me "What about this person or situation is triggering you?"

We all get triggered when we are not seen, heard, or valued. When we move into the Name step, it signals our Gentle Warrior to step forward. "Don't worry love," she whispers, "I've got a better plan for us."

Every little conflict is an opportunity to use the circumstance to proactively practice the structure of Name, Claim and Reframe: What intention do I want to bring to the situation?

Breathe deeply and Name your emotion. This allows your Gentle Warrior to receive whatever you are experiencing (anger, frustration, rejection, fear), so you can Name where you are and what you need emotionally so you can achieve a more balanced state of mind.

Claim by separating your ego from your below the line trigger and replace it with an above the line action that will help you move up and out of the mess you have encountered.

Holding on and expecting that there is only one path through will not help you deal with the situation at hand. Resistance only creates internal conflict. Stop for a moment to calm yourself: "I accept what has happened without resistance, I accept that some things are out of my control."

Reframe the whole snafu by creating a mindset that encourages optimistic, strategic, and visionary thinking. By accepting full responsibility for the role that we play in each challenge, we allow ourselves the opportunity to pivot our approach and shape-shift our mindset. The story that you tell yourself is what effectively determines your next steps moving forward. When adversity strikes, let go of any expectations you may be holding on to or the plans you have put into place. Detours are often portals to unexpected learning, some that even become blessings in disguise.

Name, Claim and Reframe is the path to embracing the gentleness that lives inside your truth, and the best part is that you can get there by choosing to proactively stand in your own power. Did you ever dream that this would be possible to achieve? I know that as women, we were taught that strong and gentle cannot be interwoven, yet we have learned that with grace, ingenuity, and the spirit of a now gentler warrior, they can. In fact, their integration can enhance our power and impact. Aren't you ready to show the world a different way through? Learning to be intentional about maintaining our heart, soul, and body is not selfish. It's carving out quiet time and then boldly justifying it so you can nurture yourself like you do everyone else—refresh, renew and replenish.

Calling Forth All Gentle Warriors!

It is time for society to recognize that the concept of masculine and feminine are not traits associated with a specific gender, but rather characteristics that we all have the power to call up when we need them. To be a balanced, poised, and confident person, we must employ the best parts of our wholeness by wielding both our masculine and feminine superpowers. I came through the ranks just like you, believing that my feminine traits were not as potent as my masculine ones and I spent most of my life denying my divine feminine so I might present myself as a stoic, powerful, and courageous woman who didn't take crap from anyone. It left me empty and very distanced from the woman I so wanted to be. When we dare ourselves to disarm by Naming, Claiming and Reframing, we are rewarded with access to the truest source of our strength, wisdom, and resourcefulness, our Gentle Warrior. Instead of adhering to the old beliefs that confident self-assured women need to be dominant and autocratic, we have expanded our perspective to call forth altruistic, humble, and versatile energy. Those who are most impactful as leaders, both women and men, dance gracefully between both their masculine and feminine assets. We must be crusaders so we can help others see that a man or woman who displays aggressive, confrontational, and controlling behavior has dipped below the line. Show me the leader that is courageous enough to show emotion, extend gratitude and cultivate a community, and I will show you a proactive influencer with an attuned vision readying the world for an expanded and empowered future.

Acknowledgements and Special Thanks

"You've always had the power my dear,
you just had to learn it for yourself."
—GLINDA THE GOOD WITCH,
WIZARD OF OZ, FRANK L. BAUM

When you make a leap of the heart to do something significant, the universe conspires to help by presenting both people and circumstance to clear a path towards success. As I write this acknowledgment I see now that this book is a true alchemy of little miracles that have solidified Name, Claim and Reframe from a small glimmer of hope to a movement with a clear vision and purpose. With a very full and grateful heart, I thank the following A-Listers for their wisdom, guidance, and support.

My trusted Sherpa, Kim O'Hara (www.kimohara.com): Thank you for teaching me to write concisely and helping me to transform this big idea into a book. You illuminated my path with foresight and humor, especially when I had lost my way.

My incredible mentors and torch lighters: Abigail Morgan Prout (www.spiral-leadership.com), Linda Martens, Tanya Geisler (tanyageisler.com) and Tricia Bolender (www.sacredpower.co). Your generosity, grace and wisdom became the inspiration for the Gentle Warrior archetype that I present in this book.

The radiant Tanya Geisler who reminded me that I have always had the capacity to drive the Porsche engine inside my soul and who graciously agreed to write this book's spectacular foreword. YOU were a divine gift presented at the perfect time.

Cherished friends and *sisters of choice*, Cathy Truesdell, MSM and Pam Pauletich: who generously gifted me not only their friendship but their powerful stories of courage, connection, transformation, and love.

My brave clients (whose tales of transformation are obscured by pseudonyms): You have been my inspiration for the genius and introspective vision that emerges when we make the choice step out of our comfort zone.

My Fairy Godmothers, Dorthy Moxley and Joan Finnie, who have sprinkled my life with pixie dust.

My parents, Rosemary and Edward, who lovingly gave me wings to fly and encouraged me to be brave and resilient so I could do hard things. I love you both with all my heart.

My husband, Bill: You are the love of my life. Thank you for being my co-pilot and the patient, steady wind beneath my wings. The best is yet to come to us!

My children, Patrick, and Katharine: You have expanded my heart in ways I never imagined possible. I am so very proud of the people who have become. May you always live in your truth.

About the Author

Andrea Mein DeWitt is an author, speaker, and life coach who helps leaders see and step into their power, their potential, and their truth. Known for her infectious energy, her career path is proof that it is never too late to transition, modify, revise, and rewrite your life story. After over thirty years as an academic, Andrea bravely shed her cloak of education and took the courageous and transformational leap into the world of coaching. *Name, Claim & Reframe: Your Path to a Well-Lived Life* is a culmination of the wisdom that she has collected through living an imperfect life and the many tools she has developed to help her coaching clients navigate life with a more attuned vision. It takes courage to live your truth, and part of living an authentic life is stepping out of your comfort zone. Her approach is to help clients gain awareness of what is working and what areas of their life may no longer serve them.

Andrea holds an M.Ed. in Reading Leadership from UC Berkeley and is a Certified Professional Coach through the International Coaching Federation and the Co-Active Training Institute. Andrea lives in the San Francisco Bay Area with her husband and their beloved yellow Labrador.

Tanya Geisler is a certified Leadership Coach, TEDxWomen speaker, and writer who teaches leaders how to combat their Imposter Complex and lead with ICONIC impact so they can achieve their ultimate goals. Her clients include best-selling authors, heads of industries, MPs, public speakers, leaders, entrepreneurs and rockstar motivators.

Notes and Sources

Introduction
Alfred Adler and Individual Psychology
Understanding Human Nature by Alfred Adler

The Essential Self is comprised of four components: spirituality, self-care, gender identity, and cultural identity. Spirituality, not religiosity, has positive benefits for longevity and quality of life, and was viewed by Alfred Adler, an Austrian physician and psychiatrist as central to holism and wellness. His 1927 publication, *Understanding Human Nature*, introduced the general public to the fundamentals of Individual Psychology.

Chapter 1: A Call to Disarm
Panache Desai
You Are Enough: Revealing the Soul to Discover Your Power, Potential and Possibility by Panache Desai

www.panachedesai.com

Panache Desai wrote: "Often the precursor to spiritual awakening is some crisis, something that cuts through the thick layers of illusion of the ego. [The event] awakens to facilitate the emergence of the transcendent beauty and joy that you could not see in the chaos and perceived limitation . . . You begin to see life with new eyes and an open heart."

Chapter 2: Balancing Your Response

Great Gatsby-style hat

A soft-brimmed hat popular after the turn of the twentieth century. It is made of eight quarter panels and is also known as a newsboy cap.

Laura Petrie capris

The Dick Van Dyke Show was an American television sitcom that initially aired on CBS from October 3, 1961, to June 1, 1966. Laura Petrie (played by Mary Tyler Moore) was an influential figure in women's fashion and put her own spin on 1960's style, experimenting with wearing, trousers on television.

"Twiggy"

In 1966, London-based model, "Twiggy" (aka Lesley Hornby Lawson) was hired to model at age of 16 and quickly became a fashion icon known for her boyish figure, false eyelashes, exaggerated eye makeup, and closely cropped pixie hairstyle.

Spirit's Compass

According to Abigail Morgan Prout, founder of Spiral Leadership, "Conscious leaders know where they are at all times in relation to this line. Above the Line can be described as conscious, open, generative, life-affirming and curious. Below the Line can be described as closed, defensive, degenerative, life-snuffing and committed to being right. Based on millennia of survival instinct, we tend to go below the line when we feel threatened, either physically or emotionally, even if the threat isn't real."

Chapter 3: Name
Joseph Campbell on Fear
I have always loved this quote, and although it is attributed to Campbell, in sourcing its origin I found that Joseph Campbell may have employed a prolix version that was modified by others. There is no doubt, however, that this expression was influenced by his familiarity with myriad mythologies. The original quote is thought to be taken from this passage: "Where you stumble, there lies your treasure. The very cave you are afraid to enter turns out to be the source of what you are looking for. The damned thing in the cave that was so dreaded has become the center."

Gay Hendricks on Genius
Gay Hendricks, author of *The Joy of Genius,* writes that for our genius to emerge we must first free up mind space from the negative thinking of our past: "The biggest barrier blocking our path to genius is fear based negative thinking. Putting an end to the habit is a powerful investment in our genius. Paradoxically, our struggle with negative thinking only ends when we declare we have no control over it."

Further Resources for Core Wounds

mosaicmagazine.ca/whats-your-core-wound/

lonerwolf.com/core-wound/

www.psychologytoday.com/us/blog/owning-pink/201008/
   whats-your-core-wound

Chapter 4: Claim
The Inner Critic/Saboteur
The Co-Active Institute (coactive.com/), where I did my coach training, defines the dissonate voice inside your head as your Saboteur, or inner

critic: "The voice is there to keep you from taking unsafe risks, but it is overcautious at a time that calls for risks the sake of change and (living) a more fulfilling life."

Co-Active Coaching: Changing Business Transforming Lives, Third
      Edition (2011)

Nine Ways to Work with the Client and NOT the Saboteur (2012)

Saboteur (2012)

Draw Out Your Gremlin!

"What is the Inner Critic?"

"What to Do, Moment to Moment, When Self Doubt Shows Up"

Playing Big-Practical Wisdom for Women Who Want to Speak Up, Create and Lead by Tara Mohr (2015)
www.taramohr.com/

somaticmovementcenter.com
What does somatic mean? "A somatic movement is one which is performed consciously with the intention of focusing on the internal experience of the movement rather than the external appearance or result of the movement. The word somatic means "of or relating to the living body," and it has long been used in medical terminology like somatic cell, somatic nervous system, somatic disorder, and somatic pain. Due to its generic definition, the term somatic can be used to describe a variety of forms of movement and healing modalities. You may have heard of somatic yoga, somatic experiencing, somatic psychology, somatic therapy, or somatic dance therapy."

Chapter 5: Preparing for The Reframe: Defining Your Core Values

Maslow's Hierarchy of Needs

Abraham Maslow's Hierarchy of Needs is a theory of motivation which states that five categories of human needs dictate an individual's behavior. Those needs are physiological needs, safety needs, love and belonging needs, esteem needs, and self-actualization needs.

Further Reading

Fulfillment and Values ©2012 The Coaches Training Institute

Six Ways to Clarify Values ©2012 The Coaches Training Institute

Discovering Client's Values: Peak Experience ©2012 The Coaches Training Institute

www.simplypsychology.org/maslow.html

www.verywellmind.com/what-is-maslows-hierarchy-of-needs-4136760

Chapter 6: Reframe

Cleo Wade on Regret

Artist/poet/author Cleo Wade said, "Regret is focusing too much on decisions made when you were still learning."

I could not find a reference for this exact quote because I heard it spoken right from the author's mouth at a book talk she gave at San Francisco's Common Club on October 18, 2019.

Where to Begin: A Small Book About Your Power to Create Big Change in Our Crazy World by Cleo Wade (2019)

www.cleowade.com/

The George Burns and Gracie Allen Show

The George Burns and Gracie Allen Show was a half-hour television series broadcast from 1950 to 1958 on CBS. It starred George Burns and Gracie Allen, one of the most enduring acts in entertainment history. Their situation comedy TV series received Emmy Award nominations throughout its eight-year run.

Critic

Borrowed from the Latin word *criticus* in the late 16th century, the word traces its origin back to the Greek adjective *kritikós*, meaning "discerning, capable of judging." It predates the word referring to what a critic produces—criticism—by a few decades.

Education

The word education is derived from the Latin word "educare" which means to bring up. Another Latin word "educere", means to bring forth. Therefore, education to bring forth as well as bring up. Some theorists give a different explanation of the word "educate". They say 'e' means out of and *duco* means to lead' i.e. to educate means to lead forth or "to extract out" the best in a person.

Chapter 7: Name, Claim and Reframe: Family

Helicopter Parenting

The term "helicopter parent" was first used in Dr. Haim Ginott's 1969 book *Between Parents & Teenagers* by teens who said their parents would hover over them like a helicopter. It became popular enough to become a dictionary entry in 2011. Similar terms include "lawnmower parenting," "cosseting parent," or "bulldoze parenting."

Chapter 9: Name, Claim and Reframe: The Real World

Canonization

Tanya Geisler (*Your Impeccable Impact*) warns against what she calls the "canonization" of leaders, celebrities, or anyone whose work we admire: "It CAN be a complicated relationship: we see someone doing something we admire, then project a kind of glory onto them (which is an illusion, to be sure), then start to compare ourselves to that shine, then feel "less so," then feel ugh, and then we have nowhere to go but to try to cut them down... especially when their human flaws start to show up... Who wants THAT? Who wants to be placed on a pedestal only to get shoved off?"

Chapter 10: Managing Your Gentle Warrior

Further Reading

The Breathing Cure: Develop New Habits for a Healthier, Happier & Longer Life by Patrick McKeowan (2021)

Yoga Mind: 30 Days to Enhance Your Practice and Revolutionize Your Life from the Inside Out by Suzan Colón (2018)

A Path with Heart: A Guide Through the Perils and Promises of Spiritual Life by Jack Kornfield (1993)

When Things Fall Apart: Heart Advice for Difficult Times by Pema Chödron (2016)